## Canadian Living's Best

# Kids in the Kitchen

BY

## Elizabeth Baird

AND

The Food Writers of Canadian Living® Magazine
and The Canadian Living Test Kitchen

A MADISON PRESS BOOK
PRODUCED FOR
BALLANTINE BOOKS AND CANADIAN LIVING

| Ballantine Books | Canadian Living |
| A Division of | Telemedia |
| Random House of | Communications Inc. |
| Canada Limited | 25 Sheppard Avenue West |
| 2775 Matheson Blvd East | Suite 100 |
| Mississauga, Ontario | North York, Ontario |
| Canada | Canada |
| L4W 4P7 | M2N 6S7 |

Canadian Cataloguing in Publication Data

Baird, Elizabeth
Kids in the kitchen

(Canadian Living's Best)
"Produced for Ballantine Books and Canadian Living."
Includes index.
ISBN 0-345-39873-4

1. Cookery - Juvenile literature.  I. Title.  II. Series.

TX652.5.B34 1998          j641.5'123          C98-931338-7

EDITORIAL DIRECTOR: Hugh Brewster
PROJECT EDITOR: Wanda Nowakowska
EDITORIAL ASSISTANCE: Beverley Renahan, Rosemary Hillary
PRODUCTION DIRECTOR: Susan Barrable
PRODUCTION COORDINATOR: Donna Chong
BOOK DESIGN AND LAYOUT: Gordon Sibley Design Inc.
COLOR SEPARATION: Colour Technologies
PRINTING AND BINDING: Imprimeries Transcontinental Inc.

CANADIAN LIVING ADVISORY BOARD: Elizabeth Baird, Bonnie Baker Cowan,
Anna Hobbs, Caren King

CANADIAN LIVING'S BEST KIDS IN THE KITCHEN
was produced by Madison Press Books
which is under the direction of Albert E. Cummings

**Madison Press Books**
**40 Madison Avenue**
**Toronto, Ontario, Canada**
**M5R 2S1**

*Printed in Canada*

# Contents

*Chicken Fajitas (p. 41)*

*Quick Skillet Lasagna (p. 44)*

*Cookie Cottage (p. 82)*

# Introduction

Welcome to the kitchen — and to the exciting world of cooking! There's lots to do and lots to learn as you try out the many delicious recipes in this brand-new cookbook written especially for junior chefs like you. But we guarantee you'll also have lots of fun in the kitchen.

Because having fun is a large part of what cooking is all about — whether you do it on your own or in the company of your family or friends. Cooking also opens the door to a world of sharing. You may not know this yet, but one thing all good cooks have in common is a love of sharing what they make. Much of the fun of stirring up a big batch of fudgy brownies is having lots to pass around to all your favorite people. And when you make your first tossed salad for Sunday dinner, the compliments sure feel nice!

To get you started, ask to have a spot in the kitchen for yourself — it can be a shelf or drawer where you keep your apron, oven mitts, recipe book, notebook and pencil plus any special equipment you like to use. You can also create your own computer file of favorite recipes. Knowing your way around the kitchen is a big step in being independent. You can look after yourself — and you can also share in the responsibility of making family meals.

Once you're organized, you can also plan ahead. Check the calendar for upcoming events — bake sales, birthday parties, sleepovers, a family reunion picnic. What would you like to make for these special occasions? Choose a recipe, check the ingredient list and make up a shopping list. Then, go shopping! You'll learn how to pick the freshest fruits and vegetables in season and how to choose meats, chicken and fish. You'll also discover the amazing and delicious variety of canned goods, spices, grains, breads and cheeses just waiting to be tried. You can help plan family menus, too. And the bonus? You get to cook what you like to eat!

While cooking should always be fun, there is a serious side to it, too. The clean-hands routine, washing up after yourself, and being careful around anything hot or sharp is very important. So is checking with your parents or another responsible adult before you start to cook — so you have their permission, and help if you need it.

Cooking opens up your world to a lifetime of pleasure and learning. May you enjoy every moment you're in the kitchen, long after you're a kid.

*Elizabeth Baird*

*Pool Party Cake (p. 74)*

# Start the Day

When the day begins with breakfast, it begins better. Scientists have joined your parents in saying that if you eat breakfast, you'll be a lot smarter and a whole lot more fun to be with. And who wouldn't want to be both?

## Tortilla Egg Cups ▶

It's easier to pleat tortillas neatly into ramekins or muffin cups when the tortillas are warm and soft. Take them out of the fridge a few minutes before baking, or warm them in the microwave oven at Medium (70% power) for 10 seconds.

| | Vegetable oil | |
|---|---|---|
| 6 | 6-inch (15 cm) flour or corn tortillas | 6 |
| 1/2 cup | finely chopped sweet red pepper | 125 mL |
| 1/2 cup | finely chopped sweet green pepper | 125 mL |
| 2 tbsp | chopped fresh coriander or parsley | 25 mL |
| 6 | eggs | 6 |
| Pinch | each salt and pepper | Pinch |

**EQUIPMENT LIST**
- measuring cup
- measuring spoons
- pastry brush
- 6 deep ovenproof ramekins or muffin cups
- rimmed baking sheet
- cutting board
- small knife
- 2 small bowls
- oven mitts

1 Place oven rack in center of oven; turn on heat to 375°F (190°C).

2 With pastry brush and a few drops of oil, lightly grease ramekins. Set on baking sheet. Place softened tortilla over each ramekin; gently press into ramekin, pleating sides to fit neatly. Set aside.

3 In small bowl, stir together red and green peppers and coriander. Scoop out 1/4 cup (50 mL) and set aside. Divide the rest of the sweet pepper mixture equally among tortilla cups.

4 Break 1 of the eggs into separate small bowl; pour carefully into tortilla cup. Repeat with other 5 eggs. Sprinkle with salt and pepper.

5 Bake on baking sheet for 20 minutes or until whites are set but yolks are still runny. Wearing oven mitts, remove baking sheet from oven. Sprinkle eggs with saved red and green pepper mixture.

Makes 6 servings.

### VARIATION

● HAM-AND-CHEESE EGG CUPS: Substitute 6 thin slices Black Forest ham for the tortillas; cut into 5-inch (12 cm) rounds. Sprinkle egg cups with 1/3 cup (75 mL) shredded Cheddar or mozzarella cheese before baking.

## COOKING WITH EGGS

**How to break an egg**
● Set a medium-size mixing bowl on the counter. Hold the egg sideways in your hand and crack it smartly on the edge of the bowl. With both hands held over the bowl, break the two halves of the egg apart and let the egg drop into the bowl.

**How to remove bits of egg shell**
● If any bits of egg shell fall into the bowl, use a small piece of paper towel or one of the half egg shells to fish them out.

# Baked Egg Toasty Cups

|   | Vegetable oil |   |
|---|---|---|
| 4 | slices whole wheat bread | 4 |
| 1 tbsp | butter, softened | 15 mL |
| 4 | eggs | 4 |
| Pinch | each salt and pepper | Pinch |

1 Place oven rack in center of oven; turn on heat to 375°F (190°C). With pastry brush and a few drops of oil, lightly grease 4 muffin cups; set aside.

2 Stack bread on cutting board. With serrated knife, trim off crusts. Arrange in single layer on cutting board. With rolling pin, roll each slice to flatten to about 1/8-inch (3 mm) thickness.

3 Spread butter evenly over bread. Press bread slices, one at a time and buttered side up, into each muffin cup.

4 Bake for 10 minutes or until crisp and golden. Wearing oven mitts, remove muffin pan from oven; set on rack.

5 Break 1 of the eggs into small bowl; pour carefully into 1 toast cup. Repeat with other 3 eggs. Sprinkle with salt and pepper.

6 Wearing oven mitts, put muffin pan back into oven. Bake for 20 to 25 minutes or until whites are set and yolks firm.

Makes 4 servings.

You can make a supply of the toasty cups and have them on hand for a quick and wholesome egg breakfast any morning of the week.

**EQUIPMENT LIST**
- measuring spoons
- pastry brush
- muffin pan
- cutting board
- serrated knife
- rolling pin
- table knife
- oven mitts
- wire cooling rack
- small bowl

# Egg in a Hole with a Hat

|   | Butter |   |
|---|---|---|
| 1 | slice bread | 1 |
| 1 | egg | 1 |

1 With knife, butter bread lightly on both sides. Using cookie cutter, cut out circle in center of bread.

2 Break egg into small bowl. Heat small skillet over medium heat. Add 1/2 tsp (2 mL) butter and heat until melted. Place bread slice in skillet; carefully pour egg into hole in bread. Add bread circle to skillet.

3 Cook for 2 minutes or until egg is almost set. Slide one lifter under and second lifter over bread and flip. Cook for 1 minute longer or just until egg is set. Lift out onto plate and top with bread circle to make hat.

Makes 1 serving.

It's fun when you cook an egg and toast together in the same skillet.

**EQUIPMENT LIST**
- table knife
- 2-1/2-inch (6 cm) round cookie cutter
- small bowl
- small skillet
- 2 lifters

## BERRY GRANOLA NESTS ◄

*A layer of granola can hold yogurt or cottage cheese. Top with fresh raspberries, sliced strawberries, blueberries, bananas, nectarines, peaches or any other favorite fruit.*

● Pour 1/2 cup (125 mL) granola cereal into cereal bowl. Make a well in center. Spoon 1/3 cup (75 mL) thick plain yogurt or cottage cheese into well.

Top with 1/4 cup (50 mL) raspberries or sliced strawberries.
**Makes 1 serving.**

*(Left) Ham-and-Cheese Egg Cup (p. 6); Berry Granola Nest*

# Forty-Five-Second Scrambled Egg

Eggs are a great breakfast or snack for solo cooks.

**EQUIPMENT LIST**
- measuring spoons
- small microwaveable bowl
- forks
- cheese grater
- oven mitts

| | | |
|---|---|---|
| 1 | egg | 1 |
| 1 tbsp | milk | 15 mL |
| Pinch | each salt and pepper | Pinch |
| 1 tbsp | shredded cheese | 15 mL |

1 Break egg into small microwaveable bowl. Add milk, salt and pepper. With fork, beat lightly until yolk and white are blended.

2 Microwave at High for 30 seconds; stir with fork. Microwave at High for 15 seconds or until egg is set but still creamy.

3 Wearing oven mitts, remove bowl from microwave; stir with clean fork. Sprinkle with cheese.

Makes 1 serving.

# Skinny Omelette Roll-Up

Keep up your energy all morning with this one-minute omelette. You can add any cheese you like — Cheddar, mozzarella, Havarti and Swiss are good choices.

**EQUIPMENT LIST**
- medium mixing bowl
- measuring spoons
- fork
- 6-inch (15 cm) nonstick skillet
- pastry brush
- cheese grater
- cutting board
- wooden spatula
- small knife

| | | |
|---|---|---|
| 1 | egg | 1 |
| 1 tbsp | milk | 15 mL |
| Pinch | each salt and pepper | Pinch |
| 1/4 tsp | vegetable oil | 1 mL |
| 1 | 7-inch (18 cm) flour tortilla | 1 |
| 1 tbsp | shredded brick cheese | 15 mL |
| 1 tsp | chopped fresh parsley (optional) | 5 mL |

1 Break egg into bowl. Add milk, salt and pepper. With fork, beat until yolk and white are blended.

2 Heat skillet over medium-high heat. Using pastry brush, brush with oil. Pour in egg mixture, tilting skillet to spread egg evenly. Cook for 1 minute or until firm, using fork to prick any air bubbles that rise to surface.

3 Place tortilla on cutting board. Hold skillet over top edge of tortilla. With spatula, gently push omelette out of pan onto tortilla, pulling skillet back as omelette slides off so omelette covers tortilla.

4 Sprinkle with cheese, and parsley (if desired). Roll up.

Makes 1 serving.

# Cinnamon Toast

The nifty mix for the toast is also delicious sprinkled over hot oatmeal.

**EQUIPMENT LIST**
- measuring spoons
- measuring cup
- plastic container
- toaster
- cutting board
- table knife
- teaspoon

| | | |
|---|---|---|
| 1 | slice bread | 1 |
| 1 tsp | butter, softened | 5 mL |
| 1 tsp | Cinnamon Toast Mix (recipe follows) | 5 mL |

| CINNAMON TOAST MIX | | |
|---|---|---|
| 1/4 cup | granulated sugar | 50 mL |
| 2 tsp | cinnamon | 10 mL |

1 Toast bread. Lay on plate and spread with butter. Sprinkle with Cinnamon Toast Mix. Cut into quarters.

Makes 1 serving.

1 Pour sugar and cinnamon into plastic container and shake until blended. Store where it's handy for breakfast.

Makes enough for 12 slices of cinnamon toast.

# French-Toasted Banana Sandwich

| | | |
|---|---|---|
| 4 | slices whole grain bread | 4 |
| 1 tbsp | peanut butter | 15 mL |
| 2 | bananas | 2 |
| 2 | eggs | 2 |
| 1/3 cup | milk | 75 mL |
| 1/2 tsp | vanilla | 2 mL |
| Pinch | each cinnamon and salt | Pinch |
| 2 tsp | butter | 10 mL |

1 Lay bread on counter. Spread peanut butter over each slice. Peel bananas; place on cutting board. Cut each lengthwise into 4 slices. Cover 2 of the bread slices with bananas. Top with other slices; lightly press sandwiches together.

2 Break eggs into pie plate; add milk, vanilla, cinnamon and salt. Whisk with fork.

3 Place sandwiches in egg mixture. Soak until half of the egg mixture has been absorbed.

4 Place one lifter under and second lifter over each sandwich; press to hold sandwich together and turn. Let soak until all egg mixture is absorbed.

5 Place skillet over medium-high heat. Add butter, swirling it around pan. Add sandwiches; cook for about 3 minutes or until golden brown underneath.

6 Using two lifters as before, turn sandwiches over; cook until golden brown underneath.

Makes 2 servings.

Sandwiches for breakfast? Why not! If you don't like peanut butter, you can still make the sandwiches. Just use your favorite jam or honey instead.

**EQUIPMENT LIST**
- measuring spoons
- liquid measuring cup
- table knife
- cutting board
- pie plate
- fork
- 2 lifters or wooden spatulas
- large nonstick skillet

# Peanut Butter and Honey Waffles

| | | |
|---|---|---|
| 1-1/4 cups | whole wheat flour | 300 mL |
| 2 tsp | baking powder | 10 mL |
| 1/4 tsp | salt | 1 mL |
| 1/2 cup | smooth peanut butter | 125 mL |
| 1/4 cup | liquid honey | 50 mL |
| 2 | eggs | 2 |
| 1-1/4 cups | milk | 300 mL |
| 1 tsp | vanilla | 5 mL |
| | Vegetable oil | |

1 Measure flour, baking powder and salt into large bowl; stir together with wooden spoon.

2 In medium bowl, whisk together peanut butter and honey. Break eggs into same bowl; add milk and vanilla. Whisk together until smooth. Pour over dry ingredients. Stir just until dry ingredients are wet.

3 Heat waffle iron according to manufacturer's directions. With pastry brush, brush lightly with oil. Pour in 1/3 to 1/2 cup (75 to 125 mL) batter, depending on capacity of waffle iron. Close lid and cook for 3 to 4 minutes or until golden and crisp.

4 Using fork, spear waffle and transfer to plate. Keep pouring batter and cooking waffles until all batter has been used up.

Makes 12 waffles, enough for 4 servings.

You can also use this recipe to make pancakes. If you don't have whole wheat flour, use all-purpose instead.

**EQUIPMENT LIST**
- large mixing bowl
- measuring cups
- measuring spoons
- wooden spoon
- medium mixing bowl
- whisk
- waffle iron
- pastry brush
- fork

**TIP:** You can substitute almond butter for peanut butter. Reduce milk to 1 cup (250 mL) and add up to 1/4 cup (50 mL) more milk if necessary to make pourable batter.

# Pancakes from Scratch ▼

Pancakes are delicious for breakfast but they also hit the spot for lunch, supper and snacks, too. This batch is big, enough for 24 pancakes — but you can wrap them individually in plastic wrap, pop them into a plastic container and freeze them for a quick toaster pancake meal later in the week.

### EQUIPMENT LIST
- large mixing bowl
- dry measuring cups
- liquid measuring cup
- measuring spoons
- wooden spoon
- medium mixing bowl
- whisk
- large nonstick skillet or griddle
- lifter

| | | |
|---|---|---|
| 1-1/2 cups | all-purpose flour | 375 mL |
| 1-1/2 cups | whole wheat flour | 375 mL |
| 3 tbsp | granulated sugar | 50 mL |
| 2 tbsp | baking powder | 25 mL |
| 1-1/2 tsp | salt | 7 mL |
| 2 | eggs | 2 |
| 3 cups | milk | 750 mL |
| 3 tbsp | vegetable oil | 50 mL |
| 1-1/2 tsp | vanilla | 7 mL |

1 Measure all-purpose flour, whole wheat flour, sugar, baking powder and salt into large bowl. Stir together with wooden spoon.

2 Break eggs into medium bowl; add milk, oil and vanilla. Whisk until smooth and bubbly. Pour over flour mixture; whisk just until dry ingredients are wet.

3 Place skillet over medium-high heat. Pour in 1/4 cup (50 mL) batter, letting it spread to make pool. Pour in 3 more pools of batter, spacing them around skillet so they don't touch.

4 Cook for about 2 minutes or until bubbles on top of each pancake break but do not fill in and pancakes are golden on bottom. With lifter, turn gently and cook for about 1 minute longer or until bottom is golden.

Makes 24 pancakes.

### WHAT A NEAT IDEA!

● Use a funnel to pour the batter into a squeeze bottle. Use the bottle to make hearts, the initials of your favorite friend or numbers for birthday breakfasts. Get creative with bear paws (pour 1 large pool of batter, with 5 smaller touching circles for toes), spider webs, dog bones and cat faces complete with whiskers.

# Strawberry Cream Cheese Spread

| | | |
|---|---|---|
| 4 oz | light cream cheese | 125 g |
| 2 tbsp | strawberry jam | 25 mL |

**1** Place cream cheese in bowl. With fork, mash until smooth and softened. Add jam and mash in with fork.

Makes 1/2 cup (125 mL), enough for 8 slices of toast.

VARIATIONS

● ORANGE: Replace jam with 1 tbsp (15 mL) thawed frozen orange juice concentrate and 1 tbsp (15 mL) liquid honey.

● CINNAMON DATE: Replace jam with 2 tbsp (25 mL) finely chopped dates and 1/4 tsp (1 mL) cinnamon.

● CINNAMON RAISIN: Replace jam with 2 tbsp (25 mL) chopped raisins and 1/4 tsp (1 mL) cinnamon.

Choose your favorite flavor to add to cream cheese and enjoy on bagels, morning toast, buns or muffins.

**EQUIPMENT LIST**
- medium bowl
- fork
- measuring spoons

# Caribbean Fruit Shake

| | | |
|---|---|---|
| 1 | ripe banana | 1 |
| 1/2 cup | pineapple juice | 125 mL |
| 1/2 cup | orange juice | 125 mL |
| 1 tbsp | grenadine syrup (optional) | 15 mL |
| 1 cup | ice cubes | 250 mL |

**1** Peel banana and break into pieces. Place in blender.

**2** Pour in pineapple juice and orange juice; add grenadine syrup, if you want. Blend until smooth.

**3** Add ice cubes; blend for 1 minute or until creamy and frothy.

Makes 2 servings.

Here's an icy-cold, all-fruit drink from food writer Bonnie Stern to enjoy for breakfast or for a cool-down snack.

**EQUIPMENT LIST**
- liquid measuring cup
- measuring spoons
- blender

**TIP:** Grenadine syrup is available in the soft-drink section of the supermarket. It turns the shake a wonderful pink.

## SHAKE UP YOUR BREAKFAST!

*With a blender, some yogurt or milk and your favorite fruit, it's easy to whiz up a nourishing breakfast drink.*

**Banana Chocolate Shake**

*With a few bananas wrapped and ready in the freezer, this thick chocolaty shake is ready in a jiff.*

● Remove 1 wrapped and frozen peeled ripe banana from freezer. Unwrap and place in blender. Add 1 cup (250 mL) chocolate milk. For extra flavor, add 2 tbsp (25 mL) smooth peanut butter. Purée until smooth.

**Makes 2 servings.**

**Power Drink**

*Fruit, milk and yogurt make this one powerful glass of energy.*

● Cut 1 banana in half; peel and break into pieces. Place banana and 1/2 cup (125 mL) sliced strawberries or blueberries in blender. Add 1/2 cup (125 mL) 2% milk and 1/2 cup (125 mL) plain yogurt. Purée until smooth.

**Makes 4 servings.**

**TIP:** Always wash strawberries before removing the hull so water doesn't soak into the fruit. To remove the hull, place berries on cutting board; with small knife, cut around hull and lift out.

# Food on the Go

Filling up those hollow spots in your tummy is easy when you know your way around the kitchen — and when the quick bites are as easy and as tasty as these.

## Pizza Heroes ▶

Choose your roll — submarine, hot dog bun or short baguette — for a hero of a sandwich.

**EQUIPMENT LIST**
- cutting board
- bread knife
- pastry brush
- broiler pan
- oven mitts
- wire rack
- sharp knife
- measuring spoons
- dry measuring cups
- liquid measuring cup
- small microwaveable bowl
- spoon
- table knife
- cheese grater

| | | |
|---|---|---|
| 2 | 6-inch (15 cm) long bread rolls | 2 |
| 1 tsp | olive oil | 5 mL |
| 2 tbsp | chopped peeled onion | 25 mL |
| Quarter | sweet green pepper, seeded, cored and slivered | Quarter |
| 1/4 cup | pizza sauce | 50 mL |
| 2 | slices smoked turkey or ham (about 3 oz/90 g) | 2 |
| 1/2 cup | shredded part-skim mozzarella cheese | 125 mL |

1 Place oven rack on second rung from top. Turn on broiler for 5 minutes.

2 Place rolls on cutting board; with bread knife, cut horizontally in half. With pastry brush, brush cut sides with oil.

3 Place on broiler pan, cut side up; broil for about 3 minutes or until golden. Wearing oven mitts, remove broiler pan from oven and set on rack.

4 Place onion and green pepper in small microwaveable bowl. Microwave at High for 1 minute or until softened; set aside.

5 Transfer top halves of buns to cutting board; set aside.

6 Using spoon, spread bottom halves of buns with half of the pizza sauce. Cover with equal amounts of onion, green pepper, turkey and cheese.

7 Wearing oven mitts, return broiler pan of buns to oven. Broil for about 1 minute or just until cheese melts. Wearing oven mitts, remove pan from oven and set on rack.

8 Spread cut side of top halves of buns with remaining sauce. Sandwich with bottom halves.

Makes 2 servings.

**TIP:** Since Pizza Heroes are good hot or cold, you can make them for your lunch. Let them cool, then wrap well in plastic wrap and keep chilled until serving time.

# Tuna Bugwiches ▼

Who can resist eating a sandwich that looks like a giant insect! You can opt for other favorite soft, thick fillings — egg or salmon salad or devilled ham — and other vegetables for legs.

**EQUIPMENT LIST**
- can opener
- sieve
- medium bowl
- fork
- cutting board
- sharp knife
- bread knife
- cheese grater
- dry measuring cups
- spoon
- rubber spatula
- lemon juicer
- measuring spoons
- bread knife
- vegetable peeler

| | | |
|---|---|---|
| 8 | dinner rolls | 8 |
| Quarter | English cucumber, thinly sliced | Quarter |
| 2 | carrots | 2 |
| 16 | small lettuce leaves | 16 |
| | Vegetable pieces | |
| 2 tbsp | light mayonnaise | 25 mL |
| | | |
| | TUNA SALAD FILLING | |
| 3 | cans (each 6.5 oz/184 g) water-packed tuna | 3 |
| 6 | radishes | 6 |
| 3/4 cup | bread-and-butter pickles, chopped | 175 mL |
| 1/2 cup | light mayonnaise | 125 mL |
| 1 tbsp | lemon juice | 15 mL |
| 1/2 tsp | salt | 2 mL |

1 TUNA SALAD FILLING: Open cans of tuna. Place sieve over bowl; dump tuna into sieve to drain. Discard liquid; dump tuna into bowl. Using fork, break apart into small pieces.

2 Lay radishes on cutting board. With sharp knife, trim off tops and roots neatly. Grate on medium holes of grater. Add to tuna along with pickles, mayonnaise, lemon juice and salt. Mix well with fork: set aside.

3 Place rolls on cutting board. With bread knife, slice horizontally 1/2 inch (1 cm) from bottom. With fingers, pull out crumbs from top half, leaving 1/2-inch (1 cm) thick walls.

4 Place cucumber slices over bottom pieces of rolls; spoon on filling to make mounds. Cover with tops.

5 Peel carrots; cut into thin sticks about 3 inches (8 cm) long. You will need 48 sticks. *(Both the filled buns and carrots can be made to this point. Wrap buns separately and enclose carrot sticks in clean damp towel in plastic bag. Refrigerate for up to 4 hours.)*

6 Insert carrot sticks into filling for legs. Make two slits, one on each side of top of roll; insert lettuce leaves for wings. Decorate with vegetable pieces for eyes, antennae and other body parts, using mayonnaise to attach.

Makes 8 sandwiches.

# Hot Tuna Subs

| 1 | can (6.5 oz/184 g) water-packed tuna | 1 |
|---|---|---|
| 1/2 cup | cubed part-skim mozzarella cheese | 125 mL |
| 1/4 cup | chopped celery | 50 mL |
| 3 tbsp | light mayonnaise | 50 mL |
| 2 tbsp | sweet pickle relish | 25 mL |
| Pinch | pepper | Pinch |
| 5 | whole wheat hot dog buns | 5 |

1 Open can of tuna. Place sieve over bowl; dump tuna into sieve to drain. Discard liquid; dump tuna into bowl. With fork, break apart into small pieces.

2 Add cheese, celery, mayonnaise, relish and pepper. Toss with fork to blend flavors.

3 With bread knife, cut buns horizontally almost all the way through. Spoon equal amount of filling into each bun. Press closed; wrap in paper towel.

4 Microwave 1 bun at High for 30 seconds, or 5 buns for 2 minutes, or until cheese melts.

Makes 5 servings.

A melty tuna salad in a bun is fast food, thanks to the microwave.

**EQUIPMENT LIST**
- can opener
- sieve
- medium bowl
- fork
- cutting board
- sharp knife
- bread knife
- measuring spoons
- dry measuring cups
- spoon
- paper towel

# Sandwich Stacks

| 2 | leaves lettuce | 2 |
|---|---|---|
| 2 | whole wheat kaiser buns | 2 |
| 2 tsp | butter, softened | 10 mL |
| 1/4 cup | light cream cheese, softened | 50 mL |
| 1/2 cup | alfalfa sprouts | 125 mL |
| 2 oz | thinly sliced smoked salmon | 60 g |
| 16 | thin slices cucumber | 16 |
| Pinch | pepper | Pinch |

1 Rinse lettuce leaves under cold water; shake off water into sink. Spin lettuce in salad spinner, or pat dry with clean tea towel. Tear each leaf in half; set aside.

2 Place buns on cutting board. With bread knife, cut horizontally in half. Lay on board, cut sides up. With fingers, pull out crumbs from insides, leaving 1/2-inch (1 cm) thick walls. Reserve bread crumbs for another use.

3 Spread butter evenly over inside of bun halves. Place lettuce leaf in hollow of each half.

4 Spread equal amount of cream cheese over lettuce on bottom of each bun. Divide alfalfa sprouts in half and place each half on top of cream cheese.

5 Place salmon slices on top of sprouts. Place cucumber slices on top of salmon. Sprinkle with pepper. Place bun tops over filling to form sandwiches.

Makes 2 sandwiches.

### VARIATIONS

● EGG SALAD SANDWICH STACKS: Place 2 peeled hard-cooked eggs in small bowl. Mash with potato masher or fork. Stir in 2 tbsp (25 mL) light mayonnaise, 2 tbsp (25 mL) finely chopped celery, 1/4 tsp (1 mL) pepper and pinch of salt. Evenly layer egg salad and 2 thinly sliced radishes over lettuce on buns.

● HAM OR SMOKED TURKEY SANDWICH STACKS: Replace smoked salmon with thinly sliced ham or smoked turkey.

These layered sandwiches can be custom-built to suit the tastes of everyone in the family. Each filling makes enough for two sandwiches, but you can double the recipe for more servings.

**EQUIPMENT LIST**
- salad spinner or clean tea towel
- cutting board
- bread knife
- sharp knife
- plastic wrap

# Race Car Sandwich ▶

Cooking-school teacher Pam Collacott says fill 'er up and have fun with sandwiches for a party, or just because you enjoy making your lunch into a car!

**EQUIPMENT LIST**
- cutting board
- sharp knife
- bread knife
- small bowl
- measuring spoons
- fork
- plate
- rubber spatula
- cheese grater
- toothpicks
- plastic bag
- scissors

| 1 | small oblong bread roll or hot dog bun | 1 |
|---|---|---|
| 1 tbsp | peanut butter | 15 mL |
| 1 tbsp | grated apple | 15 mL |
| 1 tsp | raisins | 5 mL |
| Half | slice cucumber | Half |
| 1 | cherry tomato, radish or olive | 1 |
| 2 tbsp | mayonnaise | 25 mL |
| 4 | slices kiwifruit, cucumber, radish, carrot or banana | 4 |
| 2 | stuffed olive slices or grape halves | 2 |

1 Place roll on cutting board; with bread knife, cut roll horizontally in half almost all the way through. Set aside.

2 Measure peanut butter, apple and raisins into bowl; mix together with fork. Spread over cut side of bottom half of roll. Top with other half of roll; press gently to close. Place on plate.

3 With sharp knife, cut 1/2-inch (1 cm) slit crosswise in top of roll almost in center; insert halved cucumber slice for windshield. Pierce cherry tomato with toothpick; insert into roll just behind windshield for driver.

4 Using a little dab of mayonnaise as glue, attach kiwifruit slices at front and back sides for wheels. Glue on olive slices for headlights.

5 Spoon remaining mayonnaise into small plastic bag; snip a fine hole in one corner. Pressing mayonnaise into corner, pipe details onto car — racing number on hood and sides; racing stripe on trunk; headlights and tail lights; grill; driver's hair, eyes, nose and mouth.

Makes 1 serving.

# Grilled Cheese French Toast

If you think mustard is only good on hot dogs, you're in for a delicious surprise when you combine it with the mellow flavor of cheese.

**EQUIPMENT LIST**
- table knife
- measuring spoons
- wide shallow soup bowl
- small whisk
- liquid measuring cup
- waxed paper
- large nonstick skillet
- 2 lifters

| 4 | slices bread | 4 |
|---|---|---|
| 1 tbsp | Dijon mustard | 15 mL |
| 4 | slices Cheddar or Swiss cheese | 4 |
| 2 | eggs | 2 |
| 1/4 cup | milk | 50 mL |
| Pinch | each salt and pepper | Pinch |
| 2 tsp | butter | 10 mL |
| 1 tsp | vegetable oil | 5 mL |

1 Lay bread slices on counter. Divide mustard equally among slices; spread evenly with knife. Place 2 slices of cheese on 2 of the bread slices; cover with remaining slices of bread, mustard-side down. Press together lightly.

2 Break eggs into bowl; whisk until yolk and white are blended. Whisk in milk, salt and pepper.

3 Lay 1 sandwich in egg mixture. Using both lifters, one under and one on top, turn sandwich to soak both sides. Place on sheet of waxed paper. Repeat with second sandwich, letting it soak up all the remaining egg mixture.

4 Place skillet over medium heat; add butter and oil, swirling to coat surface. Lay sandwiches in skillet; cook for about 3 minutes or until golden brown underneath.

5 Using both lifters, one under and one on top, turn each sandwich. Cook for about 3 minutes longer or until golden brown underneath and cheese is melted and oozy.

Makes 2 servings.

## PEANUT BUTTER PITA BITES

*Here's a neat way to add crunchy carrots and celery to a peanut butter-stuffed pita. For variety, try the fruit and vegetables in cream cheese instead of peanut butter.*

**YOU WILL NEED:** vegetable peeler, cheese grater, cutting board, sharp knife, small bowl, fork, dry measuring cups.
● For 12 well-stuffed mini pita sandwiches, mix 1 peeled and grated carrot, 1 finely chopped stalk celery, 1/4 cup (50 mL) raisins and 2 chopped dates into 1/2 cup (125 mL) smooth or crunchy peanut butter. Slit the sides of 12 mini pita breads and use a small spoon to stuff with filling.
**Makes 2 to 3 servings.**

# Bean and Vegetable Burritos ◄

| 1 tsp | vegetable oil | 5 mL |
|---|---|---|
| 2 | onions, peeled and chopped | 2 |
| 1 | clove garlic, peeled and minced | 1 |
| 1 | sweet green pepper, seeded, cored and chopped | 1 |
| 1 | small zucchini, chopped | 1 |
| 1 | large carrot, peeled and grated | 1 |
| 2 tsp | chili powder | 10 mL |
| 1 tsp | each dried oregano and cumin | 5 mL |
| 1/4 tsp | each salt and pepper | 1 mL |
| 1 | can (14 oz/398 mL) red kidney beans | 1 |
| 1-1/2 cups | salsa | 375 mL |
| 5 | 9-inch (23 cm) flour tortillas | 5 |
| 1/2 cup | shredded Cheddar cheese | 125 mL |
| 1/2 cup | low-fat plain yogurt | 125 mL |

1 Place oven rack in center of oven; turn on heat to 400°F (200°C).

2 With pastry brush, brush skillet with oil; place over medium heat. Add onions, garlic, green pepper, zucchini and carrot; cook, stirring with spatula, for 6 minutes.

3 Add chili powder, oregano, cumin, salt and pepper; cook for 2 minutes longer or until vegetables are softened.

4 Meanwhile, open can of beans. Place sieve in sink; pour beans into sieve to drain. Rinse beans under cold water and drain well. Pour into bowl; mash beans coarsely with fork. Add half of the salsa and mix together.

5 Lay tortillas on counter. Leaving 1-inch (2.5 cm) border all around, spread each tortilla with about 1/3 cup (75 mL) of the bean mixture. Cover with vegetable mixture. Roll up tortillas. Place, seam side down, in baking dish. Bake in oven for 15 minutes.

6 Wearing oven mitts, remove baking dish from oven and set on rack. Sprinkle tortillas with cheese. Wearing oven mitts, return baking dish to oven.

7 Bake for 5 minutes or until cheese has melted and filling is piping hot. Serve with yogurt and remaining salsa.

Makes 5 servings.

For extra visual appeal, wrap up your burritos in colored tortillas — spinach green or salsa red.

**EQUIPMENT LIST**
- pastry brush
- measuring spoons
- medium nonstick skillet
- cutting board
- sharp knife
- cheese grater
- wooden spatula
- rubber spatula
- sieve
- medium bowl
- fork
- liquid measuring cup
- can opener
- 13- x 9-inch (3 L) baking dish
- oven mitts
- wire rack
- dry measuring cups

# Aloha Quesadillas

| 2 | small flour tortillas | 2 |
|---|---|---|
| 2 tbsp | pasta sauce | 25 mL |
| 2 tbsp | chopped ham | 25 mL |
| 2 tbsp | pineapple tidbits | 25 mL |
| 1/4 cup | shredded mozzarella cheese | 50 mL |

1 Lay tortillas on counter; with spoon, spread half of each one with half of the sauce. Sprinkle ham, pineapple and mozzarella on sauce. Fold uncovered half over filling.

2 Heat skillet over medium heat. Holding both ends, carefully place quesadillas, straight sides together, in skillet. Cook for about 2 minutes or until tortillas are speckled brown on bottom.

3 Using both lifters, one under and one on top, turn quesadillas. Cook for 2 minutes longer or until speckled brown underneath and cheese is melted.

Makes 2 servings.

Tortillas go Hawaiian with a tropical pineapple and ham filling.

**EQUIPMENT LIST**
- measuring spoons
- spoon
- table knife
- cutting board
- sharp knife
- dry measuring cups
- cheese grater
- medium nonstick skillet
- 2 lifters

# Green Hair and Eggs

Sprouts growing out of the top of an egg? What a great way to grow sprouts for sandwiches and have eggs for egg salad sandwiches. Look for seeds in a health food store.

**EQUIPMENT LIST**
- 2 eggs
- small saucepan
- small sharp knife
- small coffee spoon
- small bowl
- permanent colored markers
- cotton balls
- alfalfa, cress or sprouting radish seeds
- pipe cleaners

1 Place eggs in small saucepan; cover with cold water. Place over medium-high heat and bring to boil.

2 Remove from heat and let stand for 20 minutes. Carefully pour off water; fill saucepan with cold water and let eggs cool.

3 Tap lightly all around top of pointed end of egg to break shell. Break off shell about a quarter of the way down egg. With spoon, carefully scoop out egg into bowl; cover and refrigerate for salad (see Egg Salad Sandwich Stacks, p. 17). Wipe shells clean; let dry.

4 With markers, draw face on front of each shell. Fill shells with cotton balls and moisten with water.

5 Sprinkle seeds on top of cotton balls. Place shells in egg cups; set in warm spot, adding a little water every day, until seeds sprout.

6 Wrap pipe cleaner around base of each egg; shape ends to look like arms.

Makes 2 egg heads.

## PACK A PERFECT LUNCH

*Here's how to pack a lunch that stays fresh and delivers great taste and nutrition.*

1 A good lunch should have something from each of the four food groups: dairy, fruits and vegetables, whole grains and bread, and meats or alternates.

2 Choose whole grain, dark rye or pumpernickel instead of white bread. For extra fiber, pack bran muffins or whole wheat pitas or buns.

3 For sandwich fillings, include sliced cold meat leftovers from dinner, sliced turkey or chicken, part-skim or skim milk cheese, salmon and peanut butter. Choose tuna that has been packed in water, not oil.

4 Pack raw vegetables along with a dip (see p. 23). Or make a dip by adding chopped green onions, parsley, salt and pepper to smooth cottage cheese and yogurt.

5 Leftovers make great lunches. Pizza, stir-fries, pasta dishes, meat loaf, bean salad and coleslaw are good choices.

6 Treat yourself to a nutritious sweet to enjoy at the end of lunch — an oatmeal cookie, banana or carrot bread, applesauce or fresh fruit in season.

7 Pack a safe lunch. By freezing a small box of juice and packing it into a soft insulated lunch bag, or using a freezer pack, you can safely pack yogurt, cottage cheese or other dairy products.

8 Choose foods that keep safely at room temperature. In warm weather, cheese and peanut butter are good choices; avoid eggs, fish, poultry and meat.

9 Pack a hot lunch by using a wide-mouth vacuum bottle to hold chili, baked beans, spaghetti with meatballs, soup or stew.

10 Don't reuse lunch-box wrappings; they may contain bacteria.

# Pizza Potato Skins

| | | |
|---|---|---|
| 1 | large potato (about 8 oz/250 g) | 1 |
| 1 tbsp | tomato sauce or ketchup | 15 mL |
| Pinch | dried oregano | Pinch |
| Pinch | pepper | Pinch |
| 1/2 cup | shredded mozzarella cheese | 125 mL |

1 Scrub potato. Hold firmly in one hand; prick 3 times with fork. Microwave at High for 3 to 6 minutes or until tender all the way through; test with fork. Let cool for 5 minutes.

2 Wearing oven mitt and holding potato steady, cut in half lengthwise. With spoon, scoop out most of the pulp, leaving shells about 1/4 inch (5 mm) thick. Reserve pulp for another use.

3 Place potato shells on cutting board and cut each in half lengthwise; place on microwaveable plate.

4 Spread each wedge with tomato sauce; sprinkle with oregano and pepper. Top with cheese. Microwave at High for 1 to 2 minutes or until cheese melts.

Makes 1 or 2 servings.

You don't have to phone for pizza when you can microwave this quick snack, lunch or light supper.

**EQUIPMENT LIST**
- fork
- oven mitts
- sharp knife
- spoon
- measuring spoons
- cheese grater
- dry measuring cups

**TIP:** You can bake up enough potatoes for supper, with leftovers for snacks. Bake potatoes in oven or toaster oven at 450°F (230°C) for 45 minutes or until tender. To cook cheese-topped wedges, place on baking sheet and broil for 2 to 3 minutes. Be wise and use oven mitts when handling hot food.

# Pizza Knots

| | | |
|---|---|---|
| 1 | tube refrigerated pizza dough | 1 |
| 1/3 cup | tomato sauce | 75 mL |
| 1/4 tsp | dried oregano | 1 mL |
| 1/2 cup | shredded part-skim mozzarella cheese | 125 mL |

1 Place oven rack in center of oven; turn on heat to 425°F (220°C). Line baking sheet with foil; set aside.

2 Unroll dough, keeping rectangular shape. Lay flat on cutting board. Cut in half lengthwise; cut into 8 crosswise strips, making 16 small strips.

3 Stretch and twist each strip into rope shape; tie loosely in knot.

4 Place knots on baking sheet; using pastry brush, brush with tomato sauce. Sprinkle with oregano and cheese.

5 Bake for 15 minutes or until golden. Wearing oven mitts, remove baking sheet from oven. Using lifter, transfer knots immediately to rack and let cool.

Makes 16 knots.

Hot or cold, these snacks are delish. Save leftovers for packed lunches.

**EQUIPMENT LIST**
- baking sheet
- aluminum foil
- cutting board
- sharp knife
- pastry brush
- liquid measuring cup
- dry measuring cup
- measuring spoons
- cheese grater
- oven mitts
- lifter
- wire rack

# Tzatziki

This all-purpose dip is wonderful with vegetables or pita wedges.

**EQUIPMENT LIST**
- new or clean J-cloth or cheesecloth
- rubber spatula
- liquid measuring cup
- medium sieve
- medium bowl
- small sieve
- small bowl
- vegetable peeler
- measuring spoons
- cheese grater
- cutting board
- sharp knife
- spoon

| 1-1/3 cups | plain yogurt | 325 mL |
|---|---|---|
| One-third | English cucumber | One-third |
| 1/2 tsp | salt | 2 mL |
| 2 tsp | each olive oil and lemon juice | 10 mL |
| 1 | clove garlic, minced | 1 |
| 1/2 tsp | pepper | 2 mL |

1 Line medium sieve with J-cloth or double thickness of cheesecloth. Place sieve over medium bowl; with spatula, scrape yogurt into sieve to drain.

2 Place sieve and bowl in refrigerator; let yogurt drain for at least 3 hours or until it has shrunk to about 3/4 of its former amount (about 1 cup/250 mL). Discard clear liquid in bowl.

3 Meanwhile, peel cucumber; grate against coarse holes of grater. Place in small sieve set over small bowl; sprinkle with salt. Set aside to drain for 1 hour.

4 Squeeze cucumber lightly; pour off drained water. Return cucumber to bowl.

5 Add thickened yogurt, oil, lemon juice, garlic and pepper. With spoon, stir well to combine.

Makes 1 cup (250 mL).

**TIP:** For a change, try Tzatziki spooned on sliced tomatoes or chicken breasts or slathered in fish, beef or veggie burgers.

# Peanut Butter Dip

Double the pleasure of fresh fruit with this smooth and creamy dip.

**EQUIPMENT LIST**
- sharp knife
- cheese grater
- dry measuring cups
- liquid measuring cup
- medium bowl
- wooden spoon
- rubber spatula
- small serving bowl
- cutting board
- serving plate

| 1/2 cup | finely grated peeled carrot | 125 mL |
|---|---|---|
| 1/2 cup | crunchy peanut butter | 125 mL |
| 1/4 cup | orange juice | 50 mL |
| 1 | each apple, pear and banana | 1 |

1 Measure carrot, peanut butter and orange juice into medium bowl; stir with spoon to combine. With spatula, scrape into serving bowl. Cover with plastic wrap and refrigerate for about 1 hour or until cold.

2 On cutting board and using sharp knife, cut apple and pear into quarters from stem end down. Cut around core and remove. Place fruit quarters flat on cutting board; cut in half lengthwise to make 8 wedges.

3 Peel banana: cut into thumb-size pieces. Place dip in center of serving plate and surround with fruit.

Makes 6 to 8 servings.

**TIP:** For the best dippers, choose firm fruit such as strawberries or slices of apples, pears, nectarines, peaches and bananas.

# Veggies and Dip ▼

| | | |
|---|---|---|
| 1 | bunch broccoli, cut in florets | 1 |
| 3 | stalks celery, cut in sticks | 3 |
| 3 | carrots, cut in sticks | 3 |
| 2 | sweet red peppers, cut in sticks | 2 |
| 1 | cucumber, cut in sticks | 1 |
| | Cherry tomatoes | |
| | **HERB DIP** | |
| 1 cup | 2% plain yogurt | 250 mL |
| 1 cup | light sour cream | 250 mL |
| 1 | clove garlic, peeled and minced | 1 |
| 3 tbsp | chopped fresh parsley | 50 mL |
| 2 tbsp | each chopped fresh chives and thyme | 25 mL |
| 1 tbsp | Dijon mustard | 15 mL |
| 1/4 tsp | each salt and pepper | 1 mL |
| 1 tbsp | lemon juice | 15 mL |

1 Wrap broccoli, celery, carrots, red peppers and cucumber individually in paper towels and enclose in separate plastic bags. Store in refrigerator for up to 1 day.

2 HERB DIP: Measure yogurt and sour cream into bowl. Add garlic, parsley, chives, thyme, mustard, salt and pepper; stir with spatula. Cover with plastic wrap and refrigerate.

3 Stir lemon juice into dip just before serving. With spatula, scrape dip into serving bowl. Arrange vegetables on platter; arrange cherry tomatoes in center. Serve dip alongside.

Makes 12 servings.

N ext time the gang gathers at your house, here's an easy way to munch on something healthy. For instructions on cutting up vegetables, see p. 43.

**EQUIPMENT LIST**
- cutting board
- vegetable peeler
- sharp knife
- dry measuring cups
- paper towels
- plastic bags
- rubber spatula
- large bowl
- measuring spoons
- serving bowl and plate

## Porcupine Ball ▲

Use the vegetable quills to scoop up the cheese. Pretzel sticks can replace all or some of the vegetables. If you like, divide cheese in half and make two balls.

**EQUIPMENT LIST**
• dry measuring cups
• rubber spatula
• medium bowl
• cheese grater
• plastic wrap
• salad spinner
• small serving plate
• vegetable peeler
• cutting board
• sharp knife

| | | |
|---|---|---|
| 1/2 cup | light cream cheese, softened | 125 mL |
| 1/2 cup | shredded Cheddar cheese | 125 mL |
| 1 | leaf lettuce | 1 |
| 2 | raisins or currants | 2 |
| 1 | slice radish, halved | 1 |
| 1 | carrot, peeled | 1 |
| 1 | stalk celery, trimmed | 1 |

1 With spatula, scrape cream cheese into bowl; add Cheddar cheese and mix together.

2 Lay sheet of plastic wrap on counter. Scrape cheese mixture onto center of plastic wrap; bring up sides and twist at top. Holding twist, mould cheese mixture into oval shape, narrowing one end for head.

3 Place lettuce on plate. Unwrap cheese onto lettuce. Set in raisins for eyes. Press cut sides of radish into cheese for mouth.

4 Cut carrot and celery into pencil-thin finger-length sticks. Push into cheese mixture to make quills.

Makes 6 to 8 servings.

**TIP:** To make ahead, do not insert vegetable quills. Cover ball completely with plastic wrap and refrigerate for up to 2 days. Let stand at room temperature for 5 minutes before serving. Add vegetable quills.

# Applesauce

| 4 | apples | 4 |
|---|--------|---|
| 2 tbsp | water | 25 mL |
| 1 tbsp | (approx) granulated sugar | 15 mL |
| 1/4 tsp | cinnamon | 1 mL |

1 With vegetable peeler, peel apples; place on cutting board. With sharp knife, cut in half from stem end down. Lay flat side down; cut into quarters. Trim out core; chop apples coarsely.

2 Place apples and water in saucepan. Cover and place on medium heat. Bring to boil, reduce heat to low and cook for 10 minutes. Wearing oven mitts, lift lid and stir twice. Apples are cooked when they look clear, start to foam and are tender when pricked with fork.

3 Remove saucepan from heat and set on rack; mash apples with potato masher. Stir in sugar and cinnamon. Taste, adding a little more sugar if you like.

4 With spatula, scrape applesauce into bowl; cover and refrigerate until cold.

Makes 3 to 4 servings.

If you like applesauce, you can make twice as much. Just double the ingredients and cook the apples a little longer.

**EQUIPMENT LIST**
- vegetable peeler
- cutting board
- sharp knife
- medium saucepan with tight-fitting lid
- wooden spoon
- measuring spoons
- oven mitts
- fork
- potato masher
- rubber spatula
- bowl

**TIP:** You can make applesauce in the microwave. Here's how: Place the apples and 1 tbsp (15 mL) water in a microwaveable casserole. Cover and microwave at High for 4 minutes; uncover, stir, cover again and microwave for 3 to 4 minutes more or until apples are tender. Mash, spice, and sweeten as above.

# Fruity Parfait

| 3/4 cup | applesauce | 175 mL |
|---------|-----------|--------|
| 2 cups | plain yogurt or vanilla pudding | 500 mL |
| 4 | maraschino cherries | 4 |

1 Using about half of the applesauce, spoon into glasses. Using about half of the yogurt, spoon over applesauce.

2 Repeat layers of applesauce and yogurt. Top each parfait with cherry. Refrigerate if making ahead.

Makes 4 servings.

Layer your parfait with applesauce or with sliced peaches, strawberries or your favorite chopped fruits.

**EQUIPMENT LIST**
- liquid measuring cup
- dessert spoon
- 4 parfait glasses
- rubber spatula

## SNACKS ON THE RUN
*Here are some fast fixes to keep you on the go.*

● **Tortilla or Pita Sandwich:** Spread tortilla with cream cheese or peanut butter; top with pineapple pieces, sliced bananas, strawberries, raisins and/or sunflower seeds and roll up. Or spread and fill pita half.

● **Apple with Peanut Butter:** Halve an apple and core with melon baller. Fill hollow with peanut butter and sprinkle with crispy rice cereal.

● **Pita Pizza:** Slice curved top off pita bread round. Spread tomato sauce inside pocket, then fill pocket with shredded mozzarella cheese, and chopped pepperoni if desired. Freeze in airtight containers to heat when required.

● **Cheese Celery Sticks:** Mix together cream cheese, shredded Cheddar cheese and a little dry mustard; stuff into celery sticks and sprinkle with some finely chopped toasted pecans.

# Microwave Orange Pudding

The microwave oven is the easiest and most reliable way to make a smooth custard pudding. Kiwi adds a fresh chunkiness, but you can use any favorite fresh or drained canned fruit.

### EQUIPMENT LIST
- 4-cup (1 L) microwaveable liquid measuring cup
- measuring spoons
- small whisk
- oven mitts
- medium bowl
- rubber spatula
- cheese grater
- liquid measuring cup
- cutting board
- sharp knife

| | | |
|---|---|---|
| 1 cup | milk | 250 mL |
| 2 tbsp | granulated sugar | 25 mL |
| 2 tbsp | cornstarch | 25 mL |
| Pinch | salt | Pinch |
| 1 | egg | 1 |
| 2 tsp | grated orange rind (optional) | 10 mL |
| 1/4 cup | orange juice | 50 mL |
| 1/2 tsp | vanilla | 2 mL |
| 1 | kiwifruit | 1 |

1 Pour milk into 4-cup (1 L) measuring cup; add sugar, cornstarch and salt. Whisk until smooth. Microwave at High for 90 seconds.

2 Wearing oven mitts, remove measuring cup from microwave and whisk. Repeat microwaving and whisking twice more or until pudding has thickened.

3 Break egg into bowl; whisk until smooth. Whisking constantly, gradually add about half of the pudding to egg. Scrape back into measure; whisk to blend.

4 Microwave at High for 30 seconds; whisk. Microwave for 30 seconds longer or until bubbly around edge. Whisk in rind (if using), juice and vanilla. Refrigerate until chilled.

5 Meanwhile, place kiwifruit on cutting board. With sharp knife, trim off ends; peel off fuzzy skin. Cut in half lengthwise; slice each half crosswise. Add to chilled pudding.

Makes 2 servings.

## CHILL OUT WITH YOGURT

*You'll be the coolest kid on the block when you invite friends over to share in these deliciously easy slushy treats.*

### Frosty Fruit Yogurt

Whiz together frozen fruit and yogurt for a slushy treat that's best eaten right away.

**YOU WILL NEED:** 4 fruit dishes, dry measuring cups, food processor or blender, rubber spatula.

● Place fruit dishes in freezer to chill. Meanwhile, measure 3 cups (750 mL) individually frozen unsweetened strawberries or mixed fruit into food processor. Put on cover and whirl until fruit is coarsely chopped.

● Add 3/4 cup (175 mL) plain yogurt and 1/3 cup (75 mL) granulated sugar; using on/off motion, pulse just until yogurt and fruit are blended. Spoon into chilled dishes.

**Makes 4 servings.**

### Yogurt Pops

Use a different juice concentrate to create a new flavor each time you make these cool treats.

**YOU WILL NEED:** dry measuring cup, rubber spatula, medium bowl, whisk, frozen pops moulds or small paper cups, wooden sticks.

● Measure 2 cups (500 mL) plain yogurt into bowl. Add 1 can (6 oz/170 mL) frozen sweetened juice or lemonade concentrate, thawed, (no water) and whisk to blend. Pour into frozen pops moulds or paper cups; place wooden sticks in centers. Freeze for 2 hours or until solid.

● To serve, remove pops by holding moulds under warm running water for a few seconds, or peel off paper cups.

**Makes about 12 pops.**

# Chocolate Banana Pops

| 2 oz | semisweet or milk chocolate | 60 g |
|------|------------------------------|------|
| 1 | large banana | 1 |

1 Pour 2 inches (5 cm) hot water into saucepan; heat until simmering. Place piece of waxed paper on plate; set aside.

2 Place chocolate on cutting board; chop coarsely with knife. Scoop into bowl; set bowl over saucepan. Let chocolate melt, stirring a few times with wooden spoon.

3 Wearing oven mitts, lift bowl from saucepan onto counter.

4 Peel banana; cut in half. Push wooden sticks into cut ends of each half. Holding 1 banana half by stick and using knife, spread chocolate all over banana; place on waxed paper-lined plate. Repeat with second banana half.

5 Freeze on plate for 1 hour. Serve immediately or wrap well in plastic wrap and store in freezer for a few days.

Makes 2 servings.

A banana coated in chocolate? You've gotta try it!

**EQUIPMENT LIST**
- cutting board
- sharp knife
- medium heatproof bowl
- small saucepan
- wooden spoon
- oven mitts
- 2 wooden sticks
- table knife
- waxed paper
- plate

# Jelly Belly Melons

| 1 | honeydew or cantaloupe melon | 1 |
|------|------------------------------|------|
| 1 cup | finely chopped fresh fruit (peaches, berries, grapes, bananas) | 250 mL |
| 1 cup | clear fruit juice (such as cranberry, apple or grape) | 250 mL |
| 1-1/2 tsp | unflavored gelatin | 7 mL |

1 Place melon, stem end up, on cutting board; with sharp knife, cut melon in half from stem end down. Scoop out seeds and discard.

2 Trim thin slice of rind from each bottom to steady halves; place on tray. Fill each melon cavity with chopped fruit.

3 Pour juice into saucepan; sprinkle with gelatin and let stand for 5 minutes. Heat over low heat, stirring, until gelatin dissolves. Do not allow to boil. Let cool; pour over fruit in melon cavity.

4 Place tray with melons in refrigerator for about 1 hour or until chilled and gelatin has set. Cut each melon half into 2 wedges.

Makes 4 servings.

This refreshing summer snack or dessert is pretty enough for a party.

**EQUIPMENT LIST**
- cutting board
- sharp knife
- spoon
- small tray
- dry measuring cups
- measuring spoons
- small saucepan
- wooden spoon
- liquid measuring cup

# Trail Mix

| 2 cups | corn-and-bran cereal squares | 500 mL |
|------|------------------------------|------|
| 1-1/2 cups | multigrain cereal circles | 375 mL |
| 1 cup | raisins | 250 mL |
| 1/2 cup | almonds | 125 mL |
| 1/2 cup | sliced dried apricots | 125 mL |
| 1/3 cup | pumpkin seeds | 75 mL |

1 Measure cereal squares, cereal circles, raisins, almonds, apricots and pumpkin seeds into large bowl; with wooden spoon, mix well.

2 Spoon into plastic bags, or cover bowl with plastic wrap, and store for up to 3 days.

Makes 6 cups (1.5 L).

Careful! This crunchy mix is addictive!

**EQUIPMENT LIST**
- dry measuring cups
- large bowl
- wooden spoon
- plastic bags or plastic wrap

# Super Suppers

With these easy-to-make main dishes, you're sure to shine in the kitchen — and win family raves at the table. Just don't tell anyone how easy it really is when you follow the recipe!

## Chicken Fingers with Dipping Sauce ▶

Here's delicious proof from food writer Bonnie Stern that homemade chicken fingers are even better than the fast-food ones.

| | | |
|---|---|---|
| 1 tbsp | vegetable oil | 15 mL |
| 40 | soda crackers | 40 |
| 1/3 cup | mayonnaise or light mayonnaise | 75 mL |
| 4 | boneless skinless chicken breasts | 4 |
| | DIPPING SAUCE | |
| 3 tbsp | ketchup | 50 mL |
| 3 tbsp | plum sauce | 50 mL |
| 1 tsp | soy sauce | 5 mL |

1 Place oven rack in center of oven; turn on heat to 400°F (200°C). Brush baking sheet with oil; set aside.

2 Place crackers in plastic bag; close bag and roll rolling pin firmly over bag until crackers are in fine crumbs. Measure to make sure there are 1-1/2 cups (375 mL) crumbs. Crush more if needed. Pour into pie plate. Scrape mayonnaise into medium bowl. Set crumbs and mayonnaise aside.

3 Place chicken on cutting board. Using sharp knife, cut each breast crosswise into 4 or 5 strips; pat dry with paper towels. Add to bowl of mayonnaise; using tongs, turn to coat strips evenly all over.

4 With tongs, transfer chicken strips, one at a time, to cracker crumbs, turning and patting crumbs all over chicken. Arrange strips so they don't touch on baking sheet.

5 Bake for 15 minutes. Wearing oven mitts, remove baking sheet from oven; using lifter, turn strips over. Bake for 15 to 20 minutes longer or until coating is golden and crisp and chicken is no longer pink inside when cut with paring knife.

6 DIPPING SAUCE: Meanwhile, measure ketchup, plum sauce and soy sauce into small bowl. Stir with spoon. Place in center of serving platter. Arrange chicken strips around bowl.

Makes 4 servings.

**EQUIPMENT LIST**
- rimmed baking sheet
- pastry brush
- plastic bag
- rolling pin
- dry measuring cups
- measuring spoons
- pie plate or shallow dish
- medium bowl
- rubber spatula
- cutting board
- sharp knife
- paper towels
- tongs or fork
- oven mitts
- lifter
- paring knife
- small bowl
- spoon
- serving platter

**PREPARING RAW CHICKEN**

As soon as you have finished preparing raw chicken or any other meat or fish, wash your hands with soap and warm water. Place plastic cutting board and all equipment you used in the dishwasher. Wash your hands again. Or, handwash everything in hot soapy water and rinse in hot water. Let dry.

# Chicken Finger Wraps ▼

Tender chicken, crunchy peppers and a silky sauce make an ideal supper or meal on the go. If you have time, make your own tzatziki (recipe, p. 24); otherwise, store-bought is fine.

**EQUIPMENT LIST**
- rimmed baking sheet
- aluminum foil
- cutting board
- sharp knife
- plate
- medium bowl
- measuring spoons
- rubber spatula
- tongs or fork
- oven mitts
- table knife

| | | |
|---|---|---|
| 1 | sweet red or green pepper | 1 |
| 1 lb | boneless skinless chicken breasts | 500 g |
| 2 tbsp | soy sauce | 25 mL |
| 1 tbsp | Dijon mustard | 15 mL |
| 1/4 tsp | pepper | 1 mL |
| 4 | 10-inch (25 cm) flour tortillas | 4 |
| 1 cup | tzatziki | 250 mL |
| 4 | leaves Boston or leaf lettuce | 4 |

1 Line baking sheet with foil; set aside. Place oven rack in top broiling position in oven. Turn on broiler a few minutes before broiling chicken.

2 On cutting board and using sharp knife, cut red pepper into strips; set aside on plate. Cut chicken lengthwise into finger-size strips.

3 Measure soy sauce, mustard and pepper into bowl; add chicken and toss with tongs to coat strips evenly all over. Arrange in single layer on baking sheet.

4 Broil for 5 to 7 minutes or until chicken is no longer pink inside when cut with clean sharp knife. Wearing oven mitts, remove baking sheet from oven.

5 Place tortillas on clean counter. Spread each one with about 3 tbsp (50 mL) tzatziki. Top with lettuce leaf. Divide chicken and red pepper strips among tortillas, arranging strips vertically in center of each tortilla.

6 Fold bottom of tortilla up over bottom of strips; fold one side into center and overlap with opposite side. (*You can wrap the tortillas tightly in plastic wrap and refrigerate them for up to 3 hours.*)

Makes 4 servings.

# Fruity Glazed Chicken Wings

| | | |
|---|---|---|
| 1 tbsp | vegetable oil | 15 mL |
| 2-3/4 lb | chicken wings (about 16) | 1.4 kg |
| 1/4 tsp | each salt and pepper | 1 mL |
| | GLAZE | |
| 1/4 cup | frozen orange juice concentrate, thawed | 50 mL |
| 3 tbsp | liquid honey | 50 mL |
| 1 tbsp | soy sauce | 15 mL |
| 1 tbsp | peach or apricot jam or orange marmalade | 15 mL |
| 1/4 tsp | ginger | 1 mL |
| 1 | clove garlic, peeled and minced | 1 |
| Dash | Worcestershire sauce | Dash |
| Pinch | salt | Pinch |

1 Place oven rack in center of oven; turn on heat to 400°F (200°C). Line baking sheet with foil; brush lightly with oil and set aside.

2 Working with 1 wing at a time, stretch wing out on cutting board. With sharp knife, cut off tip at the joint. Throw tip away. Cut remaining 2 sections in half through the joint (where it's easier to cut).

3 Arrange wing pieces without touching on baking sheet. Sprinkle with salt and pepper. Bake for 15 minutes. Wearing oven mitts, remove baking sheet from oven; use tongs to turn wings over. Bake for 15 minutes longer.

4 GLAZE: Meanwhile, measure orange juice concentrate, honey, soy sauce, jam, ginger, garlic, Worcestershire sauce and salt into bowl. Stir well.

5 Wearing oven mitts, remove baking sheet from oven and set on rack. Tilt baking sheet carefully to let fat gather in corner; spoon off fat into container (discard fat when cold). Brush both sides of wings with glaze.

6 Return wings to oven; bake for about 10 minutes or until wings are crisp and brown. Test wings with tip of clean knife (juices inside must be clear).

Makes 4 servings.

This glaze is delicious on thighs and drumsticks, too.

**EQUIPMENT LIST**
- rimmed baking sheet
- aluminum foil
- pastry brush
- cutting board
- sharp knife
- tongs or fork
- measuring spoons
- liquid measuring cup
- rubber spatula
- medium bowl
- spoon
- oven mitts
- lifter
- wire rack

## KEEP IT CLEAN WHEN COOKING

- Before starting to cook, roll up your sleeves. Tie back your hair if it's long.
- Wash your hands well. Experts recommend 30 seconds of soaping and sudsing both sides of your hands and getting under the nails with a brush. Just count to see how long that is!
- If you lick your fingers, or blow your nose or handle raw meat, poultry, fish or eggs with your hands while cooking, wash your hands again.
- Wear an apron and tie the strings in front so you can slip a clean tea towel over the strings. Use the towel for wiping hands as you work.
- Keep a separate cutting board for meat, poultry and fish. A small plastic one that fits into the dishwasher is ideal. No dishwasher? Wash the board, knives and anything else that you used while preparing these ingredients in hot sudsy water to which you've added a capful of bleach. Rinse well and let dry on a rack.
- If anything spills on the floor or counter, wipe it up immediately. Use a clean dish cloth on counters; for floors, use paper towels or scrub cloths that go right into the laundry. Slippery floors are dangerous, and spills elsewhere harden and are more difficult to clean up later.
- Wash up as you go along. Rinse dishes, wash in hot sudsy water, rinse again and let dry on racks.

# Baked Chicken Dinner ▲

Cooking a whole dinner in one dish — potatoes, carrots and chicken — will make you a star at home.

**EQUIPMENT LIST**
- pastry brush
- 16-cup (4 L) shallow casserole dish
- vegetable peeler
- cutting board
- sharp knife
- liquid measuring cup
- measuring spoons
- aluminum foil
- oven mitts
- wooden spatula
- tongs

| | | |
|---|---|---|
| 1 tbsp | vegetable oil | 15 mL |
| 4 | large carrots | 4 |
| 4 | potatoes | 4 |
| 2/3 cup | chicken stock | 150 mL |
| 3/4 tsp | salt | 4 mL |
| 1/2 tsp | pepper | 2 mL |
| 4 | chicken breasts (about 1-1/2 lb/750 g) | 4 |
| 1/4 cup | Dijon mustard | 50 mL |
| 1/2 tsp | dried thyme | 2 mL |

1 Place oven rack in center of oven; turn on heat to 400°F (200°C). Lightly brush casserole dish with oil; set aside.

2 Peel carrots. On cutting board and using sharp knife, cut into thin strips. Spread evenly in prepared baking dish.

3 Peel potatoes; cut into 1-1/2-inch (4 cm) pieces. Spread in baking dish to make layer of vegetables.

4 Pour half of the stock over vegetables. Sprinkle with 1/4 tsp (1 mL) each of the salt and pepper. Cover with foil, shiny side down. Bake for 25 minutes. Reduce heat to 375°F (190°C).

5 Wearing oven mitts, remove casserole from oven. Uncover and stir vegetables with spatula.

6 Using tongs, nestle chicken among vegetables. Whisk remaining salt and pepper, mustard and thyme into remaining stock. Pour over chicken.

7 Bake, uncovered, for 45 minutes or until vegetables are tender and chicken is golden brown outside and no longer pink inside. Check with tip of small sharp knife to see that juices in chicken run clear.

Makes 4 servings.

# Chicken Surprise

| | | |
|---|---|---|
| 3 tbsp | vegetable oil | 50 mL |
| 2 | eggs | 2 |
| 1/2 cup | all-purpose flour | 125 mL |
| 1 cup | dry bread crumbs | 250 mL |
| 6 | boneless skinless chicken breasts | 6 |
| | Salt and pepper | |
| 3 | thin slices ham | 3 |
| 3 | thin slices Cheddar cheese | 3 |
| 6 | lemon wedges | 6 |

1 Place oven rack in center of oven; turn on heat to 400°F (200°C). Line baking sheet with foil; brush lightly with a little of the oil and set aside.

2 Break eggs into one pie plate; with fork, beat until egg whites and yolks are well mixed. Scatter flour into second pie plate and bread crumbs into third. Set all aside.

3 Working with 1 chicken breast at a time, place, shinier side down, on cutting board. With fingers, locate thin fillet or tenderloin; pull away from rest of the breast. (You can wrap and freeze these for a stir-fry, p. 36, or for chicken finger wraps, p. 32.)

4 Cover remaining chicken with sheet of waxed paper. Pound with flat side of mallet or small saucepan until evenly thin, about 1/4 inch (5 mm). Sprinkle lightly with salt and pepper.

5 Cut each slice of ham and cheese in half to fit on one half of chicken piece; place on chicken. Brush edge of chicken around ham and cheese with egg. Fold uncovered side over; press edges to seal.

6 Hold chicken by both ends; dip into flour. Turn to coat both sides. Gently shake off any excess.

7 Next, dip into eggs, turning over to coat. Place flat in bread crumbs. With fingertips, press chicken into crumbs. Turn over to coat other side. Place in single layer on baking sheet.

8 Drizzle chicken with remaining oil. Bake for 25 to 30 minutes or until crispy and brown on outside, and neat cut with sharp knife reveals that chicken is no longer pink inside. Serve with lemon wedges.

Makes 6 servings.

This is chicken cordon bleu from food writer Bonnie Stern, a delicious "haute cuisine" dish that's fun to pound, bread and stuff with the surprise.

**EQUIPMENT LIST**
- aluminum foil
- rimmed baking sheet
- pastry brush
- fork
- 3 small pie plates or shallow dishes
- cutting board
- sharp knife
- waxed paper
- wooden mallet

## SAFETY IN THE KITCHEN

- Before you start, make sure it's OK for you to cook. Let an adult know what you're cooking and what ingredients and equipment you're using.
- An adult's help is necessary when you're using sharp knives, the stove, microwave, food processor, blender or any other gadget that heats up or comes with a blade.
- Keep electric cords off the stove top and on the counter, not dangling over the edge.

- Always cut on a cutting board and point knives and peelers down and away from yourself. Place a rubber non-skid pad or damp dish cloth under the cutting board so it doesn't move as you chop and cut.
- Point pot handles toward the center of the stove so no one bumps into them, and knocks them off the stove, on their way past.

- Always wear oven mitts or use pot holders when taking something out of the oven, off the stove or out of the microwave.
- Make sure you have cooling racks ready on the counter to hold hot dishes or baking sheets.
- Before you leave the kitchen, make it a habit to check that the oven and stove are both turned off.

# Chicken Stir-Fry and Rice

Timing the various dishes that make up a menu is one of the trickiest parts of cooking. With instructions for cooking the rice right in this easy stir-fry recipe, you won't have any trouble getting everything to the table on time.

**EQUIPMENT LIST**
- vegetable peeler
- cutting board
- sharp knife
- liquid measuring cup
- measuring spoons
- small bowl
- spoon
- medium saucepan with tight-fitting lid
- fork
- large wok or nonstick skillet
- wooden spatula or spoon
- plate

| | | |
|---|---|---|
| 3 | carrots | 3 |
| Half | small cauliflower | Half |
| 2 cups | snow peas | 500 mL |
| 1 lb | boneless skinless chicken breasts | 500 g |
| 1/4 cup | low-sodium soy sauce | 50 mL |
| 3 tbsp | vinegar | 50 mL |
| 3 tbsp | liquid honey | 50 mL |
| 1 tbsp | cornstarch | 15 mL |
| 1/4 tsp | salt | 1 mL |
| 1-1/3 cups | long-grain rice | 325 mL |
| 2 tbsp | vegetable oil | 25 mL |
| 1 cup | bean sprouts | 250 mL |

1 Peel carrots. On cutting board and using sharp knife, cut into thick slices. Cut cauliflower into bite-size pieces. Cut snow peas in half crosswise. Set vegetables aside.

2 On cutting board and using sharp knife, cut chicken breasts crosswise into pencil-thin strips; set aside on cutting board.

3 In small bowl, stir together soy sauce, vinegar, honey and cornstarch until cornstarch is dissolved. Set aside.

4 In saucepan, bring 2-2/3 cups (650 mL) water and salt to boil; with wooden spatula, stir in rice. Cover with lid and reduce heat to low; simmer for 20 minutes without lifting lid or until rice is tender and liquid is absorbed. Stir gently with fork to fluff. Turn off heat.

5 While rice is simmering, place wok over medium-high heat. Pour in half of the oil; swirl wok until oil covers bottom and side.

6 Heat oil; add half of the chicken. Stir-fry for about 5 minutes, lifting chicken up from the bottom with wooden spatula and tossing, until browned and no longer pink inside. Lift chicken onto plate. Repeat with remaining chicken.

7 Add remaining oil to wok; add carrots and cauliflower. Stir-fry for 5 minutes or until vegetables begin to soften.

8 Stir soy sauce mixture; pour into wok. Bring to boil, stirring constantly; cook for 2 minutes or until sauce is thickened and vegetables are glazed.

9 Add chicken, snow peas and bean sprouts; stir for about 2 minutes or until snow peas are bright green and tender-crisp.

10 Divide rice evenly among 4 dinner plates or shallow bowls. Spoon stir-fry over top.

Makes 4 servings.

**VEGETABLES IN STIR-FRIES**
Instead of the vegetables listed in a stir-fry recipe, you can substitute other family favorites. Always cook dense, hard vegetables such as carrots, cauliflower and onions longer than thin, quick-cooking ones such as snow peas, green beans, sliced broccoli and sweet peppers. Add the quick-cooking vegetables near end of recipe and cook briefly.

# Mini Meat Loaf Muffins

| | | |
|---|---|---|
| 2 | green onions | 2 |
| 1 | carrot | 1 |
| 1 | egg | 1 |
| 1/4 cup | dry bread crumbs | 50 mL |
| 1-1/2 tsp | dried basil | 7 mL |
| 1 tsp | Dijon mustard | 5 mL |
| 1/2 tsp | salt | 2 mL |
| 1/4 tsp | pepper | 1 mL |
| 1 lb | lean ground beef | 500 g |
| 3 tbsp | chili sauce | 50 mL |

1 Place oven rack in center of oven; turn on heat to 375°F (190°C).

2 On cutting board and with sharp knife, thinly slice onions. Peel carrot and grate coarsely. Place onions and carrot in large bowl.

3 Break egg into same bowl; add bread crumbs, basil, mustard, salt and pepper. Mix well with fork. Add beef; mix with hands.

4 Divide mixture into 6 parts; with hands, form into 6 balls, wetting hands in cold water if they get too sticky. Place balls in muffin pan; spoon on chili sauce.

5 Bake for 20 to 25 minutes. Wearing oven mitts, remove pan from oven; with tip of pointed knife, check 1 meatball. If it is no longer pink inside, meatballs are cooked. (Return to oven if beef is still pink.)

Makes 4 servings.

Here's a recipe that will help get supper on the table fast.

**EQUIPMENT LIST**
- sharp knife
- cutting board
- vegetable peeler
- cheese grater
- large bowl
- dry measuring cups
- measuring spoons
- fork
- rubber spatula
- muffin pan

# Scalloped Franks and Taters

| | | |
|---|---|---|
| 1 tbsp | vegetable oil | 15 mL |
| 4 | large potatoes | 4 |
| 2 | large onions | 2 |
| 6 | frankfurters, sliced | 6 |
| 2 tbsp | chopped fresh parsley | 25 mL |
| 1/4 cup | shredded Cheddar cheese | 50 mL |
| | SAUCE | |
| 3 tbsp | butter | 50 mL |
| 2 tbsp | all-purpose flour | 25 mL |
| 1/2 tsp | salt | 2 mL |
| 1/4 tsp | pepper | 1 mL |
| 2 cups | milk | 500 mL |

1 Place oven rack in center of oven; turn on heat to 400°F (200°C). Brush baking dish lightly with oil; set aside.

2 Fill large saucepan half-full with water; cover and bring to boil over high heat.

3 Meanwhile, scrub potatoes (peel, if you like); on cutting board and with sharp knife, cut into slices to make 4-1/2 cups (1.125 L). Peel and slice onions.

4 Add potatoes and onions to boiling water; boil for 5 minutes. Place colander in sink. Wearing oven mitts, carry pan carefully to sink and pour out vegetables and water into colander. Let drain.

5 SAUCE: Place medium saucepan over medium heat; add butter and melt. With wooden spoon, stir in flour, salt and pepper; cook, stirring, for 1 minute. With one hand, pour in milk and with the other, whisk mixture vigorously. Increase heat to medium-high. Cook for 5 minutes, whisking constantly, until sauce is boiling and thickened slightly.

6 Spread one-third of the potato mixture in baking dish. Top with half of the frankfurters and parsley. Wearing oven mitts and using spatula to guide the sauce, pour one-third of the sauce over top. Repeat layers, ending with sauce. Sprinkle with cheese.

7 Bake for 30 to 45 minutes or until bubbling and golden brown on top.

Makes 4 servings.

Potatoes go main-course with a creamy sauce and frankfurters (wieners). Use any kind of wiener or, if you like, chopped ham or smoked chicken or turkey instead.

**EQUIPMENT LIST**
- 11- x 7-inch (2 L) glass baking dish
- pastry brush
- large saucepan with tight-fitting lid
- vegetable scrubbing brush
- cutting board
- sharp knife
- dry measuring cup
- oven mitts
- colander
- medium saucepan or 8-cup (2 L) liquid measuring cup
- wooden spoon
- wire whisk
- measuring spoons
- cheese grater
- rubber spatula

# Crunchy Fish Burgers ▶

An oven-baked fish fillet nestled in a bun with all the trimmings is a lot easier to make than it looks. And it's impressive, too!

**EQUIPMENT LIST**
- 3 shallow bowls
- measuring spoons
- small whisk
- plastic bag
- rolling pin
- cutting board
- sharp knife
- tongs
- rimmed baking sheet
- fork
- lifter
- bread knife
- small bowl
- spoon
- small knife
- oven mitts

| | | |
|---|---|---|
| 1 tbsp | (approx) vegetable oil | 15 mL |
| 2 tbsp | all-purpose flour | 25 mL |
| 1/2 tsp | dried basil | 2 mL |
| 1/2 tsp | salt | 2 mL |
| 1/4 tsp | pepper | 1 mL |
| 1 | egg | 1 |
| 2 cups | corn flakes | 500 mL |
| 1 lb | fish fillets | 500 g |
| 1/4 cup | light mayonnaise | 50 mL |
| 2 tbsp | pickle relish | 25 mL |
| 1/2 tsp | lemon juice | 2 mL |
| Dash | hot pepper sauce | Dash |
| 4 | whole wheat hamburger buns | 4 |
| 4 | lettuce leaves | 4 |
| 2 | tomatoes | 2 |

1 Place oven rack in center of oven; turn on heat to 450°F (230°C). Brush baking sheet with a little of the oil; set aside.

2 Measure flour, basil, salt and pepper into shallow bowl. Break egg into second bowl and add remaining oil; whisk until yolk and white are blended.

3 Measure corn flakes into plastic bag; lay on counter and crush with rolling pin until in coarse crumbs. Empty crumbs into third shallow bowl.

4 Lay fish on cutting board; with sharp knife, cut into 4 pieces that match size and shape of rolls. Place baking sheet beside fish and bowls.

5 Using tongs, dip fish, one piece at a time, into flour mixture, shaking it to let excess flour drop off. Then dip into egg, turning fish over so all sides are coated and holding it above the bowl for a few seconds at the end to let extra egg drip off.

6 Lay fish in crushed corn flakes; turn over. With fingers, press crumbs onto all sides of fish. Place fish on baking sheet.

7 Bake for about 8 minutes or until golden and crisp and fish flakes easily when fork is inserted in center.

8 While fish is baking, measure mayonnaise, pickle relish, lemon juice and hot pepper sauce into small bowl; stir together with spoon. Set aside.

9 Wash cutting board. Using bread knife, slice buns in half horizontally. Open up on serving plates. Spread one side with mayonnaise sauce. Cover with lettuce. Using small knife, slice tomatoes.

10 Wearing oven mitts and using lifter, place fish fillet on each lettuce-topped bun. Top with tomato slices. Top with remaining bun.

Makes 4 servings.

## IT HELPS TO BE ORGANIZED

● Read the recipe through before beginning to cook.
● Set out all the ingredients before you start. Put them on one side of the counter, then move them over to the left as you use them. That way, you can doublecheck that you've added everything.

● Get out all the equipment and utensils you'll need for the recipe, and make sure each is the right size. There's nothing worse than seeing your pan overflowing with batter!
● Put away all the ingredients and equipment when you're finished.

● Plan how to serve the dish you're making. Choose a serving platter or dish that suits the food and arrange the food nicely. It's always a good idea to add a garnish, even if it's only a sprinkle of parsley on a soup or a dusting of icing sugar on a cake.

# Chicken Fajitas ◄

| | | |
|---|---|---|
| 1 | avocado | 1 |
| 1 | lime | 1 |
| 6 | 10-inch (25 cm) flour tortillas | 6 |
| 1 | each sweet red, green and yellow pepper, cored and seeded | 1 |
| 1 | onion, peeled and sliced | 1 |
| 1 | zucchini, trimmed | 1 |
| 4 | cloves garlic, peeled and minced | 4 |
| 1 tsp | ground cumin | 5 mL |
| 3/4 tsp | each salt and pepper | 4 mL |
| 1 lb | boneless skinless chicken breasts | 500 g |
| 1-1/2 tsp | chili powder | 7 mL |
| 2 tbsp | vegetable oil | 25 mL |
| 1 tsp | Dijon mustard | 5 mL |
| 2 tbsp | chopped fresh coriander (optional) | 25 mL |

1 On cutting board, cut avocado in half. Holding each half steady, twist out pit with fork. With spoon, scoop avocado flesh into small bowl. Mash with fork.

2 Cut lime in half crosswise; press and twist on juicer to squeeze out juice. Pour juice over avocado and mix well with fork; set aside.

3 Wrap tortillas in foil. Heat oven or toaster oven to 350°F (180°C). Just before cooking the vegetables and chicken, place foil packet of tortillas into oven to warm.

4 On cutting board and using sharp knife, slice red, green and yellow peppers into pencil-thin strips.

5 Place onion, peppers, zucchini and half of the garlic in medium bowl. Sprinkle with cumin and half of the salt and pepper; toss well to spread seasonings evenly over vegetables. Set aside.

6 Lay chicken breasts on cutting board; cut crosswise into thin strips. Place in another bowl; sprinkle with chili powder and remaining salt and pepper. Toss well.

7 Place skillet over medium-high heat. Add 1 tbsp (15 mL) of the oil. Heat until a drop of water sizzles in skillet. Add half of the chicken; let brown. Turn with wooden spatula and brown on other side.

8 Remove one piece; cut in half with knife. If the chicken is no longer pink inside, it is done. Remove to clean plate. Add remaining chicken and repeat cooking.

9 Add remaining oil to skillet. Add reserved vegetables; cook, stirring almost constantly, for about 6 minutes or until onion is softened and remaining vegetables are tender-crisp.

10 Return chicken and any juices to skillet; heat briefly until chicken is hot. Add coriander (if using) and mustard; toss well to combine flavors. Remove from heat.

11 Wearing oven mitts, remove tortillas from oven. Lay tortillas on clean counter. Spread each tortilla with equal amount of avocado mixture. Divide chicken and vegetables among tortillas; roll up.

Makes 6 servings.

Something as good as fajitas has to be shared, so try them out on the family. It doesn't hurt to invite a helper to slice the vegetables and mash the avocado while you tend the skillet.

**EQUIPMENT LIST**
- cutting board
- sharp knife
- small bowl
- spoon
- fork
- juicer
- 2 medium bowls
- measuring spoons
- tongs
- large nonstick skillet
- wooden spatula
- plate
- aluminum foil
- toaster oven
- table knife

**TIP:** Most avocados need to ripen before using. Three or four days before making fajitas, let firm avocado ripen on counter out of sunlight until it yields to gentle touch. Rough-skinned Haas avocados turn dark green, almost black, when ripe.

# Vegetarian Chili

Two kinds of lentils plus squash, tomatoes and peppers make this chili absolutely delicious and nutritious. Try it over a baked white or sweet potato, over rice or couscous or served in a bowl with toasted bagels or buns alongside.

**EQUIPMENT LIST**
- Dutch oven with lid
- measuring spoons
- wooden spoon
- dry measuring cups
- liquid measuring cup
- can opener
- cutting board
- sharp knife
- vegetable peeler

| | | |
|---|---|---|
| 1 tbsp | vegetable oil | 15 mL |
| 2 tbsp | chili powder | 25 mL |
| 1 tbsp | dried oregano | 15 mL |
| 1 tsp | each ground cumin and coriander | 5 mL |
| 1 tsp | each salt and pepper | 5 mL |
| 1 | large sweet red or green pepper, chopped | 1 |
| 1 | large red onion, peeled and chopped | 1 |
| 3 | stalks celery, sliced | 3 |
| 3 | large cloves garlic, peeled and minced | 3 |
| 1/2 cup | green lentils | 125 mL |
| 1/2 cup | red lentils | 125 mL |
| 1 | can (19 oz/540 mL) tomatoes | 1 |
| 3 cups | cubed peeled butternut squash | 750 mL |

1 Place Dutch oven over medium heat; pour in oil. With wooden spoon, stir in chili powder, oregano, cumin, coriander, salt and pepper. Cook, stirring, for 1 minute.

2 Add red pepper, onion, celery and garlic; cook, stirring often, for about 8 minutes or until vegetables are softened.

3 Stir green and red lentils into pan; cook for 3 minutes. Add 4 cups (1 L) water; bring to boil. Reduce heat to low; cover with lid and simmer for 15 minutes or until vegetables are fork-tender and green lentils have begun to soften.

4 Open can of tomatoes; add to Dutch oven. With wooden spoon, break tomatoes into chunks. Stir in squash. Simmer, uncovered and stirring often, for 30 minutes or until vegetables and lentils are tender and liquid is thickened.

*Makes 6 servings.*

# All-Vegetable Pasta

Using only one pot to cook the pasta, vegetables and sauce makes for an easy clean-up.

**EQUIPMENT LIST**
- large pasta pot with lid
- measuring spoons
- colander
- vegetable peeler
- cutting board
- sharp knife
- dry measuring cups
- liquid measuring cup
- cheese grater

| | | |
|---|---|---|
| 2-1/2 tsp | salt | 12 mL |
| 12 oz | fettuccine or linguine pasta | 375 g |
| 2 | large carrots, peeled and thinly sliced | 2 |
| 1-1/2 cups | frozen peas | 375 mL |
| 3/4 cup | milk | 175 mL |
| 1/4 cup | cream cheese | 50 mL |
| 1 cup | shredded Cheddar cheese | 250 mL |
| 3/4 tsp | dried basil (or 1/4 cup/50 mL chopped fresh) | 4 mL |
| 1/4 tsp | pepper | 1 mL |

1 Fill large pot with about 16 cups (4 L) water. Add 2 tsp (10 mL) of the salt and cover. Place over high heat and bring to boil.

2 Add pasta; press down as it softens until pasta is completely under boiling water. Boil, stirring occasionally, for 5 minutes.

3 Add carrots; cook for 5 minutes. Add peas; cook for 1 minute or until pasta and carrots are tender but still a little firm.

4 Place colander in sink. Wearing oven mitts, carefully drain pasta and vegetables into colander. Shake colander; leave in sink to drain.

5 Return pot to medium heat; add milk and heat until steaming. Add cream cheese, stirring until sauce is smooth. Return pasta and vegetables to pot. Add Cheddar cheese, basil, remaining pepper and salt; stir until well combined.

*Makes 4 servings.*

# HOW TO PREPARE VEGETABLES

*Here's how to prepare vegetables for cooking or for eating raw.*

### Broccoli

- Place broccoli on cutting board. With sharp knife, cut stalk in half crosswise just below the florets. Trim leaves and end from stalk; peel with vegetable peeler.
- Cut in half lengthwise; with flat side down, cut into sticks. Gather sticks together and cut in half. Use for dipping or steaming.
- Separate florets into bite-size pieces, keeping tiny stalks attached to florets.

### Butternut Squash

- Place squash on cutting board. Steady with one hand; cut in half just above the rounded part. Trim or break off stem. Place top half, cut side down, on board. Cut in half from top to bottom. Peel with vegetable peeler.
- Place bottom half, cut side down, on board; cut in half from top to bottom. With spoon, scoop out seeds; peel with vegetable peeler.

- With flat side down on board, cut squash pieces into finger-size strips, then gather strips together. Holding them firmly in one hand, cut crosswise into neat cubes.

### Carrots

- Using vegetable peeler, peel carrots; place on cutting board. With sharp knife, trim off stem end. Cut carrots crosswise into slices about as thick as a loonie.

### Cauliflower

- Trim all leaves and cut out core from cauliflower. Cut in half from top to core end. Break into florets or cut into bite-size pieces.

### Celery

- Trim root end and any blemishes from celery. For slices, cut stalks in half lengthwise, then crosswise. Stack stalks neatly; slice thinly across all stalks at once.
- For celery sticks, cut lengthwise into finger-width strips. Bunch strips together and cut into finger-length strips for dipping.

### Cucumbers

- Peel field cucumber with vegetable peeler; leave skin on English cucumber.
- To cut into slices, place on cutting board; with sharp knife and holding cucumber steady, cut crosswise into slices about the thickness of a loonie.

- To cut into sticks, cut cucumber into finger-length chunks; cut in half lengthwise. With flat side down and holding knife parallel to board, cut lengthwise in half, then cut into finger-thick sticks.

### Garlic

- Place garlic cloves on cutting board; press hard on each clove with flat blade of knife. Tear off garlic peel; with knife, cut into lengthwise strips, then crosswise into fine pieces.

### Green Onions

- On cutting board and using small knife, cut off root ends of onions and any limp parts. Cut onion in half lengthwise; turn cut side down on board. Cut into slices about as thick as a loonie.

### Mushrooms

- Place mushrooms on cutting board. With small sharp knife, trim ends. Cut in half from top through stem end. Lay flat side down and slice lengthwise thinly.

### Onions

- Trim off top of onion; peel onion, leaving on root end. Turn root end down and cut in half from top to bottom.
- Lay flat side down on cutting board; make 5 parallel cuts from top to, but not through, root end. Slice crosswise into neat chunks, discarding root end.

### Potatoes

- Scrub potatoes, even if you're going to peel them. Use a paring knife to trim away any brown bits. For baked potatoes, potato salad and new potatoes, you don't need to peel skin. Peel older potatoes (the kind used most of the year).
- If peeled potatoes are large, place them on cutting board. Cut in half, then cut again into quarters. For oven fries, cut potato halves lengthwise into about 4 wedges.
- Prepare sweet potatoes in the same way.

### Snow Peas

- With small knife, trim stem end from snow peas almost all the way through. Using stem as handle, pull down fibrous spine like a zipper. For smaller pieces, cut snow peas in half crosswise.

### Sweet Peppers

- Place pepper on cutting board. With sharp knife, cut around stem of pepper; pull out stem. Cut pepper in half lengthwise; shake out seeds. Trim out white membranes.
- Place pepper, shiny skin side down, on cutting board; cut into pencil-thin strips. Gather strips together; cut crosswise into little squares.

### Zucchini

- Place zucchini on cutting board. With sharp knife, trim off ends. Cut crosswise into slices about as thick as a loonie.

# Quick Skillet Lasagna ▶

Here's a shortcut pasta supper that delivers all the great flavors of lasagna in no time at all.

### EQUIPMENT LIST
- large pasta pot with lid
- measuring spoons
- slotted spoon
- colander
- oven mitts
- large nonstick skillet
- aluminum foil
- pastry brush
- dry measuring cups
- cutting board
- sharp knife
- wooden spatula
- dessert spoon
- cheese grater

| | | |
|---|---|---|
| 1 tbsp | salt | 15 mL |
| 4 cups | rotini pasta (about 12 oz/375 g) | 1 L |
| 1 tsp | vegetable oil | 5 mL |
| 2 | zucchini, cubed | 2 |
| 1 | onion, peeled and chopped | 1 |
| Half | sweet red or green pepper, diced | Half |
| 4 cups | sliced mushrooms | 1 L |
| 1-1/2 cups | diced cooked ham | 375 mL |
| 1 tsp | dried oregano | 5 mL |
| 1/4 tsp | pepper | 1 mL |
| 1 | jar (375 mL) chunky pasta sauce | 1 |
| 1 | tub (475 g) light ricotta cheese | 1 |
| 2 cups | shredded part-skim mozzarella cheese | 500 mL |

1 Fill large pot with 16 cups (4 L) water. Add salt and cover. Place over high heat and bring to boil. Add pasta; stir well with slotted spoon. Boil, stirring occasionally, for 6 minutes.

2 To test for doneness, use slotted spoon to remove 1 rotini; taste. If pasta is tender but still firm, it is ready. Place colander in sink. Wearing oven mitts, carefully drain pasta into colander. Shake colander; leave in sink to drain.

3 Meanwhile, place oven rack in top broiling position in oven. Turn on broiler a few minutes before broiling lasagna.

4 Wrap handle of skillet with two layers of foil. Brush surface with oil; place over medium-high heat.

5 Add zucchini, onion, red pepper, mushrooms, ham, oregano and pepper. Cook, stirring with wooden spatula, for 8 minutes or until vegetables are tender.

6 Pour in pasta sauce; simmer for 5 minutes, stirring occasionally. Add pasta; stir well, then smooth surface.

7 With dessert spoon, place dollops of ricotta all over surface of pasta, spreading evenly. Sprinkle with mozzarella.

8 Broil for 5 minutes or until cheese is bubbling and golden brown. Wearing oven mitts, remove skillet from oven.

Makes 6 servings.

## GET CREATIVE WITH MAC AND CHEESE

*Next time you reach for a box of macaroni and cheese dinner, why not turn a packaged product into a healthy meal that delivers great taste — and great nutrition, too.*

### Veggie Light
● Prepare 1 pkg (225 g) macaroni and cheese dinner according to directions, reducing butter or margarine to 1 tbsp (15 mL) and increasing milk to 1/2 cup (125 mL).
● Stir in 1/2 cup (125 mL) peeled grated carrot and 1 cup (250 mL) chopped broccoli florets. If you like, add 1 chopped green onion and diced quarter sweet red pepper. Heat for about 3 minutes or until steaming hot. Makes 2 to 3 servings.

### Pizza Pizzazz
● Prepare 1 pkg (225 g) macaroni and cheese dinner according to directions.
● Stir in 4 chopped green onions, 3 chopped fresh or canned tomatoes, 1 chopped sweet green pepper, 1/4 cup (50 mL) diced pepperoni (if you want), 1/2 tsp (2 mL) dried oregano and 1/4 tsp (1 mL) pepper. Heat for about 3 minutes or until steaming hot. Makes 2 to 3 servings.

### Other Tasty Add-Ins
● Drained canned tuna or salmon, cooked peas, chopped tomatoes, sliced cooked sausage, cubed ham, smoked turkey or chicken, drained and rinsed chick-peas or red kidney beans, chopped sweet red or green pepper.

# Pasta with Meatballs

Invite a kitchen buddy to join in the fun — one of you can make the meatballs, while the other makes the sauce. Presto! a supper everyone in the family will love.

### EQUIPMENT LIST
- large bowl
- cutting board
- sharp knife
- measuring spoons
- dry measuring cups
- fork
- bowl of cold water
- rimmed baking sheet
- oven mitts
- large saucepan with lid
- 2 wooden spoons
- tongs
- large pasta pot with lid
- large serving spoon

| | | |
|---|---|---|
| 1 | egg | 1 |
| 2 | green onions, chopped | 2 |
| 1/2 tsp | dried oregano | 2 mL |
| 1/2 tsp | Dijon mustard | 2 mL |
| 1/2 tsp | salt | 2 mL |
| 1/4 tsp | pepper | 1 mL |
| 12 oz | lean ground beef | 375 g |
| 1/4 cup | dry bread crumbs | 50 mL |
| 1/4 cup | (approx) freshly grated Parmesan cheese | 50 mL |
| | Terrific Tomato Sauce (recipe, next page) | |
| 4 cups | Scoobi-Do noodles or rotini | 1 L |

1 Place oven rack in center of oven; turn on heat to 400°F (200°C).

2 Break egg into bowl; beat with fork until yolk and white are well mixed. Stir in onions, oregano, mustard, salt and pepper.

3 Add beef, bread crumbs and half of the cheese. Stir with fork, mixing to break up meat and combine well.

4 Scoop meat mixture, 1 tbsp (15 mL) at a time, and roll between palms to form into balls. Wet hands in cold water if necessary to prevent sticking. Place meatballs on baking sheet.

5 Bake for 20 minutes. Wearing oven mitts, remove baking sheet from oven. To test for doneness, cut 1 meatball in half. If meatball is no longer pink inside, it's done (otherwise, return to oven to cook for a few minutes longer).

6 Pour Terrific Tomato Sauce into large saucepan. Heat over medium heat, stirring occasionally, until simmering (bubbles break on surface of sauce). With tongs, transfer meatballs to sauce; cover saucepan and cook for 10 minutes, gently stirring a few times.

7 Meanwhile, fill pasta pot with 16 cups (4 L) water. Add 1 tbsp (15 mL) salt; cover and bring to boil over high heat. With wooden spoon, stir in noodles. Cook for 8 to 10 minutes or until tender but firm to the bite.

8 Place colander in sink; wearing oven mitts, carefully drain noodles into colander. Shake colander; leave in sink to drain.

9 Add drained pasta to sauce and meatballs; stir gently with wooden spoon to coat pasta with sauce. To serve, spoon into bowls; sprinkle with remaining cheese.

Makes 4 servings.

# Terrific Tomato Sauce

| | | |
|---|---|---|
| 2 | carrots, peeled | 2 |
| 2 | cloves garlic, peeled and chopped | 2 |
| 1 | onion, peeled and chopped | 1 |
| 1 | stalk celery, chopped | 1 |
| 1 cup | sliced mushrooms (optional) | 250 mL |
| 2 tbsp | vegetable oil | 25 mL |
| 1 tsp | dried oregano | 5 mL |
| 1 tsp | dried basil | 5 mL |
| 3/4 tsp | salt | 4 mL |
| 1/2 tsp | pepper | 2 mL |
| 1/2 tsp | granulated sugar | 2 mL |
| 1 | can (28 oz/796 mL) tomatoes | 1 |
| 1/4 cup | tomato paste | 50 mL |
| 1 tbsp | balsamic or red wine vinegar (optional) | 15 mL |

1 Grate carrots against large holes of grater. Set aside with garlic, onion, celery, and mushrooms (if using).

2 Pour oil into saucepan; heat over medium heat. Add vegetables, and mushrooms (if using), oregano, basil, salt, pepper and sugar. Cook, stirring often with wooden spoon, for about 8 minutes or until vegetables are softened.

3 Open can of tomatoes. Add to vegetables along with tomato paste; break tomatoes into chunks with wooden spoon.

4 Increase heat to high; cook until boiling (bubbles break vigorously on surface), stirring often.

5 Reduce heat to medium; simmer, stirring occasionally, for about 25 minutes or until sauce is thick enough to mound on spoon. Stir in vinegar (if using).

Makes 4 cups (1 L).

Try this tasty vegetarian sauce over pasta with a sprinkle of cheese or use it on pizza. It's especially tasty with meatballs (recipe, p. 46). Add 2 cups (500 mL) drained chick-peas or red kidney beans or 1 cup (250 mL) cubed tofu to the sauce to bolster its value as a vegetarian main course.

**EQUIPMENT LIST**
- cutting board
- paring knife
- vegetable peeler
- cheese grater
- measuring spoons
- large saucepan
- wooden spoon
- can opener
- dry measuring cups

## ALWAYS MEASURE CORRECTLY

*Measuring ingredients carefully and correctly is the key to succeeding in the kitchen. Here's how.*

### What to Use
● Make sure your kitchen has a set of measuring spoons, a set of dry measures (the nesting plastic or metal ones that come in 4 or 5 sizes) and liquid measures (usually glass cups with a spout and space between the top measurement and the rim).

● If the ingredient mounds up — for example, sugar, flour, rice, cornmeal, rolled oats, bran, nuts, raisins, sour cream or shredded cheese — use the the dry measures to measure it.

● If the ingredient can be poured — for example, juices, oil or milk — use a liquid measuring cup to measure it.

### Measuring Dry Ingredients
● When using dry measures, spoon the ingredient until it's heaped, then take a knife and sweep the excess back into the container. Never — I repeat, never — shake the cup to level off sugar or flour. That just packs it down and you'll get overly sweet and dry dishes.

● That's the rule, but here's the exception. Brown sugar should be packed enough to keep its cup shape when dumped into a bowl.

### Measuring Liquid Ingredients
● When using liquid measuring cups, set the cup on the counter, pour in the ingredient, then bend down so the cup is level with your eye.

● If the liquid doesn't come exactly to the desired mark on the outside, pour a little off or add a little, as needed.

### Using Measuring Spoons
● Dip correct-size spoon into container of dry ingredient (such as spices) and level off with knife.

● For liquids such as vinegar or vanilla, hold spoon over a small bowl and fill with required amount of liquid. If any dribbles over the top, you can always pour it back into the bottle or jar.

● Never — I repeat, never — fill measuring spoons over the dish you're working on.

# Shortcut Supper Pizza ▲

When it's your turn to make supper, make it pizza-pleasing with a quick-to-make pizza and a big bowlful of salad greens. Use tortillas, pitas or a ready-made base for the crust.

**EQUIPMENT LIST**
- 12-inch (30 cm) pizza pan or large baking sheet
- dry measuring cups
- measuring spoon
- table knife
- cheese grater
- cutting board
- sharp knife
- oven mitts
- lifter
- pizza wheel cutter

| | | |
|---|---|---|
| 1 | 12-inch (30 cm) prebaked pizza base | 1 |
| 3/4 cup | pasta or pizza sauce | 175 mL |
| 1/2 tsp | dried oregano or basil | 2 mL |
| 2 cups | shredded mozzarella cheese | 500 mL |
| 2 cups | toppings (such as sliced mushrooms, green pepper, onion rings and sliced pepperoni) | 500 mL |
| 1/4 cup | freshly grated Parmesan cheese | 50 mL |

1 Place oven rack on bottom third of oven. Turn on heat to 450°F (230°C).

2 Place pizza base on pizza pan. Spread base with pasta sauce; sprinkle with oregano and about one-third of the mozzarella. Arrange toppings evenly over cheese.

3 Sprinkle remaining mozzarella evenly over toppings. Sprinkle evenly with Parmesan cheese. Bake for 10 to 12 minutes or until cheese is bubbling and base is crisp.

4 Wearing oven mitts, remove pizza pan from oven; carefully slide pizza onto cutting board. Using pizza wheel, cut into wedges.

Makes 4 servings.

## YOUR OWN PIZZERIA

*Making your own pizza is easy. You can do it the authentic way, or try some of the ready-in-minutes pizzas using bought pizza dough, already baked pizza rounds, tortillas or pita breads.*

Keep these items on hand in the fridge, freezer and cupboard and you're almost all the way there to a homemade pizza.

### In the Freezer

● Ready-made pizza bases, frozen pizza dough, English muffins, tortillas (try the spinach or salsa-flavored colored tortillas), pita bread or flatbreads.
● Pesto and grated cheeses.

### In the Refrigerator

● Parmesan cheese, mozzarella and other stringy cheeses such as provolone and Monterey Jack plus any other cheeses you like such as Havarti, Gouda, Cheddar, herbed cream cheese or fontina.
● Pepperoni or any dried salami, ham or pastrami, vegetarian pepperoni and firm tofu.

● Sweet green and red peppers, mushrooms, green and red onions, zucchini and broccoli.
● Active dry yeast.

### In the Cupboard or Pantry

● All-purpose flour, olive oil, salt, pasta or pizza sauces, dried oregano, dried basil, dried Italian herb mix, fresh garlic cloves.

● Jars of olives and marinated artichoke hearts.
● Cans of mushrooms, tuna, anchovies (yes, anchovies — try them and we know you'll like them!), chili, red kidney beans, tomatoes and red peppers.
● Keep fresh tomatoes handy on the counter, never in the fridge.

## PIZZA DOUGH FROM SCRATCH

*Try making your own pizza dough. It's fun, and much less expensive than ready-made pizza bases or store-bought frozen pizza dough.*

**1** Into a large bowl, measure 1-1/2 cups (375 mL) all-purpose flour. With wooden spoon, mix in 1 tsp (5 mL) quick-rising (instant) dry yeast and 1/2 tsp (2 mL) salt.

**2** Pour 1/2 cup (125 mL) hand-hot tap water into liquid measuring cup; add 1 tbsp (15 mL) olive oil or canola oil. Pour over flour mixture and stir until all dry ingredients are moistened and dough looks shaggy.

**3** Dust hands with flour and gather dough into ball. Dust counter generously with flour; dump dough on counter.

**4** Folding top half of dough over bottom half, push hard against double layer of dough with heels of your hands, then give dough a quarter turn.

**5** Repeat the folding, pushing and turning for about 8 minutes or until dough is smooth, springy and stretchy like an elastic band.

**6** Keep hands and counter lightly dusted with flour if dough is sticky (but the trick is not to add too much flour). As you knead, the flour absorbs moisture and dough becomes smooth.

**7** Brush dough very lightly with olive oil or canola oil and place on counter; cover with bowl and let rise for about 45 minutes or until doubled in size.

**8** Uncover and gently stretch dough (or roll with rolling pin) to a circle about 12 inches (30 cm) wide. Dust 12-inch (30 cm) pizza pan with cornmeal and place dough over top.

**9** Starting at center, gently press dough to fill pan and form a little raised rim. If dough becomes too stretchy, let it rest for a few minutes before continuing.

**Makes one 12-inch (30 cm) pizza base. Double ingredients for 2 bases.**

## PERSONAL PIZZA — PRONTO!

*Satisfy after-school and post-game hunger pangs with an instant pizza.*

● Place tortillas, whole pita breads or English muffins on baking sheet for the oven or toaster oven.
● Spread with pasta or pizza sauce and sprinkle with dried basil or oregano.

● Add whatever you find in the fridge that tickles your fancy — such as smoked ham, pastrami, sliced wieners, leftover chicken, pepperoni, green peppers, mushrooms, cubed tofu, kidney beans.

● Top with a good sprinkle of mozzarella, plus Parmesan if you like. Broil just until topping is bubbling and edges are crisp.

# Crunchy Caesar Salad

If you like bacon in your Caesar, crisp two slices in the microwave, let cool on paper towel and crumble into the salad with the croutons.

**EQUIPMENT LIST**
- medium bowl
- measuring spoons
- cutting board
- sharp knife
- rubber spatula
- small whisk
- large salad bowl
- cheese grater
- large spoon and fork
- dry measuring cups

| | | |
|---|---|---|
| 6 cups | torn romaine lettuce | 1.5 L |
| 2 tbsp | freshly grated Parmesan cheese | 25 mL |
| 1/2 cup | croutons (see box, next page) | 125 mL |
| | CREAMY DRESSING | |
| 2 tbsp | light mayonnaise | 25 mL |
| 2 tsp | lemon juice or white wine vinegar | 10 mL |
| 1 tsp | Dijon mustard | 5 mL |
| 1 tsp | water | 5 mL |
| 1/4 tsp | Worcestershire sauce | 1 mL |
| Pinch | each salt and pepper | Pinch |
| 1 | clove garlic, peeled and minced | 1 |
| 1 tbsp | olive oil | 15 mL |

1 CREAMY DRESSING: Measure mayonnaise, lemon juice, mustard, water, Worcestershire sauce, salt and pepper into medium bowl. Add garlic; whisk together. Still whisking, drizzle in oil; set aside.

2 Measure lettuce into salad bowl; with spatula, scrape dressing over lettuce. Toss until all leaves are evenly coated.

3 Sprinkle with cheese; toss again. Sprinkle with croutons.

Makes 4 servings

# Wonton Soup

Go Asian with this flavorful soup from food writer Bonnie Stern. Look for frozen wonton wrappers in Chinese grocery stores or most supermarkets.

**EQUIPMENT LIST**
- large bowl
- measuring spoons
- fork
- sharp knife
- vegetable peeler
- cheese grater
- cutting board
- rimmed baking sheet
- waxed paper
- pastry brush
- large saucepan
- slotted spoon

| | | |
|---|---|---|
| 1 tbsp | vegetable oil | 15 mL |
| 6 cups | chicken stock | 1.5 L |
| 1 tbsp | soy sauce | 15 mL |
| 1 | carrot, thinly sliced on diagonal | 1 |
| 12 | snow peas, halved diagonally | 12 |
| | WONTONS | |
| 4 oz | ground chicken | 125 g |
| 1 tsp | cornstarch | 5 mL |
| 1 tsp | soy sauce | 5 mL |
| 1/2 tsp | salt | 2 mL |
| 1/2 tsp | sesame oil | 2 mL |
| 1 tbsp | grated carrot | 15 mL |
| 1 tbsp | chopped chives or green onion | 15 mL |
| 24 | wonton wrappers | 24 |

1 Line baking sheet with waxed paper; brush lightly with oil and set aside.

2 WONTONS: In bowl and using fork, stir together chicken, cornstarch, soy sauce, salt and oil. Mix in carrot and chives. Arrange wonton wrappers in single layer on work surface; spoon 1 tsp (5 mL) chicken mixture onto center of each wrapper. Bring edges up around filling to make little pouches, squeezing edges together to seal. Place on baking sheet. Set aside.

3 In large saucepan, bring stock, soy sauce and sliced carrot to boil over medium-high heat. Reduce heat and simmer for 5 minutes. Add wontons; cook for 3 minutes.

4 Using slotted spoon, remove one wonton. Cut through with sharp knife; if wrapper is tender and chicken is no longer pink, wonton is cooked. (Continue simmering, if needed.) Add snow peas and cook for 30 seconds.

Makes 6 servings.

## MAKE-YOUR-OWN CROUTONS

*Here's how to make those wonderful crunchy bread bits. You can make lots and keep a supply handy in a jar, ready to add to any salad or to sprinkle over soup.*

● Place 4 slices of bread (crusty French or Italian is best) on cutting board. Brush lightly with oil; sprinkle with a dried herb such as oregano, basil or Italian herb seasoning.

● Cut slices crosswise, then lengthwise into cubes. Spread out cubes on baking sheet. Bake in 350°F (180°C) oven for 5 minutes.

● Wearing oven mitts, remove baking sheet from oven; turn croutons with lifter. Return croutons to oven for about 5 minutes or until golden.

# French Onion Soup

| | | |
|---|---|---|
| 1 tbsp | butter | 15 mL |
| 2 | onions, peeled and thinly sliced | 2 |
| 1 | clove garlic, peeled and minced | 1 |
| 2 tsp | granulated sugar | 10 mL |
| 1/2 tsp | dried marjoram | 2 mL |
| 1/2 tsp | pepper | 2 mL |
| Pinch | salt | Pinch |
| 4 cups | beef stock | 1 L |
| 1 tbsp | balsamic or red wine vinegar | 15 mL |
| 4 | slices French bread | 4 |
| 3/4 cup | shredded Swiss cheese | 175 mL |

1 Measure butter into large saucepan; melt over medium heat until starting to bubble. Add onions, garlic, sugar, marjoram, pepper and salt. Stir with wooden spoon until onions are coated with butter.

2 Cover pan with lid; reduce heat to medium-low. Cook, stirring occasionally, for 15 to 20 minutes or until onions are limp.

3 Pour in stock and vinegar; increase heat to high and bring to boil. Reduce heat to medium and simmer for 10 minutes.

4 Meanwhile, place oven rack on second rung from top. Preheat broiler for 5 minutes.

5 Arrange bread on baking sheet; toast under broiler until golden brown on both sides (remember to wear oven mitts when handling hot baking sheet). Set toasted bread aside.

6 Place soup bowls on clean baking sheet. Ladle soup into bowls; top with toast slices. Sprinkle cheese evenly over top.

7 Wearing oven mitts, place baking sheet of bowls under broiler; broil for about 3 minutes or until cheese is bubbly and golden.

8 Wearing oven mitts, carefully remove baking sheet from oven. To serve, place soup bowls on individual plates.

Makes 4 servings.

It's neat when your spoon breaks through the crusty top into the steaming hot soup.

**EQUIPMENT LIST**
- sharp knife
- cutting board
- measuring spoons
- large saucepan with tight-fitting lid
- wooden spoon
- liquid measuring cup
- rimmed baking sheet
- 4 ovenproof soup bowls
- oven mitts
- ladle
- cheese grater

# Patchwork Pasta Soup

There are so many good vegetables in this chunky soup that it's sure to keep you healthy and energetic.

| | | |
|---|---|---|
| 2 | boneless skinless chicken breasts | 2 |
| 1 tbsp | vegetable oil | 15 mL |
| 3 cups | water | 750 mL |
| 1 | onion, peeled and chopped | 1 |
| 2 | sweet potatoes, peeled and cubed | 2 |
| 2 cups | tricolor bow-tie or rotini pasta | 500 mL |
| 1 | potato, peeled and cubed | 1 |
| 1 | large carrot, peeled and sliced | 1 |
| 1 | stalk celery, chopped | 1 |
| 1 | can (10 oz/284 mL) chicken stock | 1 |
| 1 cup | frozen peas | 250 mL |
| 1/4 tsp | each salt and pepper | 1 mL |

1 On cutting board and using sharp knife, cut chicken lengthwise into finger-size strips. Cut strips crosswise to make cubes; set aside.

2 Pour oil into Dutch oven; heat over medium heat. Add chicken; cook, stirring often, for 5 minutes. Remove chicken to plate; set aside.

3 To Dutch oven, add water, onion, sweet potatoes, pasta, potato, carrot, celery and chicken stock; bring to boil. Reduce heat, cover and simmer for about 12 minutes or until vegetables are almost tender.

4 With wooden spoon, stir in chicken; cook for 5 minutes. Add peas, salt and pepper; cook for about 3 minutes or until vegetables are tender and chicken is no longer pink inside when cut with sharp knife.

Makes 6 servings.

# Mashed Potatoes with Cheddar

If you like mashed potatoes, you'll love these deliciously cheesy ones from food writer Bonnie Stern.

| | | |
|---|---|---|
| 6 | potatoes (2 lb/1 kg) | 6 |
| 1 tsp | salt | 5 mL |
| 3/4 cup | milk | 175 mL |
| 2 tbsp | butter | 25 mL |
| 1-1/2 cups | shredded Cheddar cheese (about 6 oz/175 g) | 375 mL |
| 1/4 tsp | pepper | 1 mL |

1 Using vegetable peeler, peel potatoes. On cutting board and using sharp knife, cut potatoes in half lengthwise. Place flat side down and cut into 2-inch (5 cm) pieces.

2 Fill large saucepan with 12 cups (3 L) water; add salt. Cover and bring to boil over high heat. Wearing oven mitts, remove lid; using slotted spoon, carefully add potatoes.

3 Reduce heat to medium-low; cover and simmer for 20 minutes or until potatoes are tender when pierced with fork.

4 About 5 minutes before potatoes are done, place milk and butter in small saucepan. Cook over medium heat until butter is melted.

5 Place colander in sink. Wearing oven mitts, carefully pour potatoes into colander to drain; return potatoes to pot. Mash with potato masher.

6 Add milk mixture, cheese and pepper; mash until smooth.

Makes 4 servings.

# Oven Fries

| 4 | large potatoes | 4 |
|---|---|---|
| 1 tbsp | vegetable oil | 15 mL |
| 1/4 tsp | paprika | 1 mL |
| 1/4 tsp | each salt and pepper | 1 mL |

1 Place oven rack in center of oven; turn on heat to 475°F (240°C).

2 With vegetable brush, scrub potatoes. Place on cutting board; with knife, remove any blemishes. Cut in half lengthwise. Place flat side down; cut each half lengthwise into 4 wedges.

3 Place in bowl; add oil, paprika, salt and pepper. Toss with spoons until wedges are evenly coated.

4 Place potatoes in single layer on baking sheet; bake for 10 minutes.

5 Wearing oven mitts, remove baking sheet from oven; turn potatoes with lifter. Return potatoes to oven for 10 minutes longer or until crisp and golden.

Makes 6 servings.

Forget frozen fries. These easy-to-make, easy-to-love fries are lower in fat than frozen — and they taste even better!

**EQUIPMENT LIST**
- vegetable brush
- sharp knife
- cutting board
- large bowl
- measuring spoons
- 2 wooden spoons
- rimmed baking sheet
- oven mitts
- lifter

## COOKING THE BASICS

*Here's how to cook basic side dishes. Remember to add ingredients carefully to boiling water and to wear oven mitts when removing pot from stove to drain pasta or potatoes.*

### Dried Pasta

| 20 cups | water | 5 L |
|---|---|---|
| 2 tbsp | salt | 25 mL |
| 1 lb | dried pasta | 500 g |

● In large covered pot, bring water and salt to full rolling boil. Stir in pasta, separating pieces; return to boil and boil, uncovered and stirring occasionally, for 8 to 10 minutes or until tender but firm. Drain well. Makes 4 servings.

### Fresh Pasta

| 16 cups | water | 4 L |
|---|---|---|
| 4 tsp | salt | 20 mL |
| 1 lb | fresh pasta | 500 g |

● In large covered pot, bring water and salt to full rolling boil. Stir in pasta, separating pieces; return to boil and boil, uncovered and stirring occasionally, for 1 to 3 minutes or until tender but firm. Drain well. Makes 4 servings.

### Rice

| 1-1/3 cups | water | 325 mL |
|---|---|---|
| Pinch | salt | Pinch |
| 2/3 cup | white or brown long-grain rice | 150 mL |

● In saucepan, bring water and salt to boil; stir in rice. Cover and reduce heat to low; simmer white rice for 20 minutes, brown rice for 40 minutes, or until rice is tender and liquid absorbed. Makes 2 cups (500 mL), enough for 2 servings.

### Boiled Potatoes

● Scrub or peel potatoes; place in large pot. Cover with boiling water; add salt (about 1 tsp/2 mL for 2 lb/1 kg potatoes). Cover and bring to boil; boil for about 20 minutes or until fork-tender. Drain and return to pot over low heat for 30 seconds to evaporate excess moisture.

### Mashed Potatoes

| 2 lb | hot boiled peeled potatoes (4 potatoes) | 1 kg |
|---|---|---|
| 1 cup | buttermilk or milk | 250 mL |
| 4 tsp | butter | 20 mL |
| 1/2 tsp | each salt and pepper | 2 mL |

● In pot, mash together potatoes, buttermilk, butter, salt and pepper until smooth. Makes 4 servings.

### Couscous

| 1-1/12 cups | water or vegetable or or chicken stock | 375 mL |
|---|---|---|
| Pinch | salt | Pinch |
| 1 cup | couscous | 250 mL |

● In saucepan, bring water and salt to boil; stir in couscous. Remove from heat; cover and let stand for 5 minutes. Fluff with fork. Makes 3 cups (750 mL), enough for 4 servings.

# I Baked It Myself

There's nothing like fresh-baked muffins, cookies or cakes — especially when you've made them yourself. Here's a beginner's course in baking. Delicious results guaranteed!

## Chocolate Carrot Cupcakes ▶

If you make cupcakes instead of a big cake, they take less time in the oven. Plus, cupcakes are all the same size — so there are no arguments about whose slice is bigger!

**EQUIPMENT LIST**
- paper muffin cups
- muffin pans for 24 cupcakes
- dry measuring cups
- 2 large bowls
- large sieve
- wooden spoon
- measuring spoons
- whisk
- liquid measuring cup
- cutting board
- sharp knife
- cheese grater
- rubber spatula
- dessert spoon
- oven mitts
- cake tester or skewer
- 2 wire racks
- small metal spatula or table knife

| | | |
|---|---|---|
| 2 cups | all-purpose flour | 500 mL |
| 2/3 cup | unsweetened cocoa powder | 150 mL |
| 2 tsp | baking powder | 10 mL |
| 1 tsp | baking soda | 5 mL |
| 1 tsp | each cinnamon and nutmeg | 5 mL |
| 1/2 tsp | salt | 2 mL |
| 1/2 tsp | ground cloves | 2 mL |
| 4 | eggs | 4 |
| 1 cup | packed brown sugar | 250 mL |
| 1 cup | vegetable oil | 250 mL |
| 3/4 cup | unsweetened applesauce | 175 mL |
| 1/2 cup | granulated sugar | 125 mL |
| 3 cups | grated carrots (about 6 large) | 750 mL |
| 2/3 cup | chopped nuts or raisins | 150 mL |
| | Vanilla Cream Cheese Icing (recipe, p. 56) | |

1 Place oven rack in center of oven; turn on heat to 350°F (180°C). Line each muffin cup with paper liner; set aside.

2 Measure flour into bowl; place sieve over bowl and add cocoa. Press through sieve with wooden spoon.

3 Add all remaining dry ingredients: baking powder, baking soda, cinnamon, nutmeg, salt and cloves. Whisk together until no longer streaky; set aside.

4 Break eggs into separate bowl. Measure in brown sugar, oil, applesauce and granulated sugar. Whisk vigorously until smooth.

5 With rubber spatula, scrape over dry ingredients; sprinkle with carrots and nuts. With wooden spoon, stir together until well mixed and you can't see any patches of white.

6 Spoon into muffin cups, dividing batter equally. Bake for 20 to 25 minutes.

7 Wearing oven mitts, remove one muffin pan from oven. Stick cake tester into center of one cupcake and lift tester out. If tester comes out clean, cupcakes are done. If not, return pan to oven and test again in 3 or 4 minutes or until cake tester inserted in center comes out clean.

8 Wearing oven mitts, remove pans from oven. Set on racks to cool completely.

9 Remove cupcakes from pans. Spoon equal-size dollops of Vanilla Cream Cheese Icing on cupcakes. With spatula, spread evenly over cupcakes.

Makes 24 cupcakes.

# Vanilla Cream Cheese Icing

Delicious cakes and cupcakes deserve a luscious icing. Cream cheese makes this one easy to spread.

**EQUIPMENT LIST**
• medium bowl
• electric mixer
• measuring spoons
• dry measuring cup
• sieve
• wooden spoon

| | | |
|---|---|---|
| 1 | pkg (4 oz/250 g) cream cheese | 1 |
| 2 tsp | vanilla | 10 mL |
| 1 cup | icing sugar | 250 mL |

1 Let cream cheese stand at room temperature for 20 minutes to soften slightly. Unwrap into bowl; add vanilla.

2 With electric mixer, beat at medium speed for about 30 seconds or until vanilla is blended into cheese and cheese is smooth.

3 Place sieve over bowl; add sugar and press through with wooden spoon. Beat at low speed for 1 to 2 minutes or until smooth and creamy.

Makes 1-1/2 cups (375 mL), enough for 24 cupcakes or one 13- x 9-inch (3.5 L) cake.

## VARIATION

● CITRUS CREAM CHEESE ICING: Omit vanilla. Add 1 tsp (5 mL) each grated orange and lemon rinds and 1-1/2 tsp (7 mL) lemon juice to cream cheese.

# Easy Chocolate Icing

This icing is ultra chocolaty — and ultra easy!

**EQUIPMENT LIST**
• dry measuring cups
• liquid measuring cup
• small saucepan
• wooden spoon
• cutting board
• sharp knife
• rubber spatula
• oven mitts
• medium bowl

| | | |
|---|---|---|
| 2 cups | chocolate chips | 500 mL |
| 1/2 cup | milk | 125 mL |
| 1/3 cup | butter | 75 mL |

1 Pour chocolate chips and milk into saucepan. Place over low heat, stirring until melted and smooth. Wearing oven mitts, remove from heat.

2 Lay butter on cutting board; with sharp knife, cut into dice-size cubes. Stir into chocolate mixture, two at a time, until smooth.

3 With rubber spatula, scrape icing into bowl; refrigerate for about 2 hours or until thick and firm enough to mound on spoon.

Makes about 2 cups (500 mL), enough for two-layer cake.

---

## EASY SUBSTITUTIONS

*What if you don't have an ingredient you need for a baking recipe? Here are some things you can substitute. The flavor may not be exactly the same but the results should still be tasty.*

● Walnuts — use pecans or raisins.
● Raisins — use dried cranberries or cherries, currants or chopped apricots or dates.
● Brown sugar — use granulated sugar.
● Milk — use skim milk powder and follow package directions.
● Lemon rind — substitute orange rind.

● Chocolate chips — chop semisweet chocolate or milk chocolate into chunks. Or use raisins.
● Buttermilk — pour 1 tbsp (15 mL) white vinegar into 1 cup (250 mL) milk. Let stand for 10 minutes.
● Almond extract — substitute vanilla extract.
● Shortening — use butter.

# One-Bowl Cake

| | | |
|---|---|---|
| 1/2 cup | (approx) shortening | 125 mL |
| 2 cups | all-purpose flour | 500 mL |
| 1-1/4 cups | granulated sugar | 300 mL |
| 4 tsp | baking powder | 20 mL |
| 1/2 tsp | salt | 2 mL |
| 1 cup | milk | 250 mL |
| 1 tsp | almond extract | 5 mL |
| 3 | eggs | 3 |
| 2-1/2 cups | sweetened flaked coconut | 625 mL |
| | Easy Chocolate Icing (recipe, p. 56) | |

1 Place oven rack in center of oven; turn on heat to 350°F (180°C). With pastry brush and a little of the shortening, grease cake pans thoroughly on bottom and side.

2 Using pans as guide, cut out circles of waxed paper the same size as bottom of pans. Place in pans; set aside.

3 Measure flour, sugar, baking powder and salt into bowl; whisk to combine. Pour 3/4 cup (175 mL) of the milk over dry ingredients. Add remaining shortening and almond extract.

4 With electric mixer, beat wet and dry ingredients together at medium speed for 1 minute (don't worry about lumps). Add remaining milk.

5 Break eggs into small bowl; check for shells. Add eggs to batter; with electric mixer, beat for 1 minute or until batter is smooth.

6 Sprinkle 1 cup (250 mL) coconut over batter; fold in gently. Scrape into prepared pans, dividing batter equally. Bake for 30 to 40 minutes.

7 Wearing oven mitts, remove one cake pan from oven; stick cake tester into center of one layer. If tester comes out clean, cake is done. If not, return pan to oven for 3 or 4 more minutes or until tester comes out clean. Set pans on racks to cool for 5 minutes.

8 Run blade of knife around inside of each pan to loosen sides of cakes. Wearing oven mitts, lift one pan off rack. Place rack over top of pan and, holding pan and rack firmly in both hands, flip pan and rack over. Set rack back on counter; lift off pan.

9 Repeat with second pan. Let cakes cool completely. Peel off paper.

10 Place one layer, flat side up, on flat serving plate. Spoon about one-quarter of the icing on top. With palette knife, spread icing almost to edge of cake.

11 Place second layer, flat side up, on icing. Spread thin layer of icing all over cake. Let dry for a few minutes. Spread remaining icing evenly over cake. Sprinkle with remaining coconut.

Makes 10 servings.

Whether it's for a class bake sale, a birthday party or Sunday dinner, an easy-to-make cake is always a winner.

**EQUIPMENT LIST**
- pastry brush
- two 9-inch (1.5 L) round cake pans
- large bowl
- dry measuring cups
- measuring spoons
- whisk
- liquid measuring cup
- electric mixer
- wooden spoon
- rubber spatula
- small bowl
- oven mitts
- cake tester or skewer
- 2 wire racks
- palette knife or table knife

**TIP:** To keep the plate clean while you're icing the cake, use 4 strips of waxed paper. Cut them about 12 x 4 inches (30 x 10 cm) and lay them across the plate before setting down the bottom cake layer. When you've finished icing the cake, simply pull out the strips.

# Strawberry Banana Sundae Cake

This is a summer-occasion cake — for a birthday, homecoming or just a fun ending to a weekend dinner. Best of all, you can make it ahead and have it ready in the freezer.

**EQUIPMENT LIST**
- pastry brush
- 10-inch (3 L) springform pan
- waxed paper
- scissors
- measuring spoons
- small saucepan
- wooden spoon
- dry measuring cups
- large spoon
- rubber spatula
- ice cream scoop
- plastic containers
- small knife
- blender
- 1-cup (250 mL) jar with screw top
- plastic wrap
- large airtight plastic container

| 3 tbsp | butter | 50 mL |
|---|---|---|
| 1-1/2 cups | fine chocolate wafer crumbs | 375 mL |
| 3 tbsp | granulated sugar | 50 mL |
| 4 cups | vanilla frozen yogurt or ice cream | 1 L |
| 4 cups | strawberry frozen yogurt or ice cream | 1 L |
| 2 | bananas | 2 |
| | SAUCE | |
| 3 cups | strawberries | 750 mL |
| 3 tbsp | granulated sugar | 50 mL |
| 2 tbsp | orange juice | 25 mL |
| | GARNISH | |
| 1 | banana | 1 |
| 8 | strawberries | 8 |

1 With pastry brush and a little butter, lightly grease bottom of springform pan. With scissors, cut strip of waxed paper to fit neatly all around inside of pan from bottom to rim; place in pan. Set pan aside.

2 Measure butter into saucepan; melt over low heat. Remove from heat; add wafer crumbs and sugar, stirring well to blend ingredients.

3 With rubber spatula, scrape into springform pan. Spread crumbs evenly over bottom of pan; press firmly. Refrigerate for 30 minutes.

4 Meanwhile, transfer vanilla frozen yogurt to refrigerator and let soften for about 30 minutes. Scrape onto crust and spread evenly. Freeze for 2 hours or until firm.

5 SAUCE: Meanwhile, with sharp knife, remove green hull from strawberries; dump strawberries into blender. Add sugar and orange juice; buzz until smooth. Pour about half of the strawberry sauce into jar; cover and refrigerate.

6 Let strawberry frozen yogurt soften in refrigerator for 20 minutes. Peel bananas; slice and arrange over vanilla frozen yogurt. Spread with strawberry frozen yogurt.

7 Spread remaining strawberry sauce over top of cake. Return cake to freezer for about 4 hours or until firm. (To make ahead, wrap pan well with several layers of plastic wrap; place in large airtight container and store in freezer for up to 2 days).

8 Transfer cake from freezer to serving plate. Release spring on pan and remove side; remove paper. Place cake in refrigerator to soften for 30 minutes.

9 GARNISH: Slice banana and arrange around top edge of cake. Remove hulls from strawberries and slice in half. Arrange strawberries, tips up, in two circles inside bananas. Serve with reserved strawberry sauce.

Makes 16 servings.

**TIP:** When serving, dip knife in warm water between each cut and wipe off.

# Scones with Currants ▼

| 2-1/4 cups | all-purpose flour | 550 mL |
|---|---|---|
| 2 tbsp | granulated sugar | 25 mL |
| 2-1/2 tsp | baking powder | 12 mL |
| 1/2 tsp | baking soda | 2 mL |
| 1/2 tsp | salt | 2 mL |
| 1/2 cup | cold butter | 125 mL |
| 1/2 cup | currants | 125 mL |
| 1 cup | buttermilk | 250 mL |
| 1 | egg | 1 |

1 Place oven rack in center of oven; turn on heat to 425°F (220°C). Sprinkle baking sheet lightly with flour; set aside.

2 Measure flour, sugar, baking powder, baking soda and salt into large bowl; whisk until well blended.

3 Place butter on cutting board; with knife, cut lengthwise, then crosswise, to make dice-size cubes. Sprinkle over dry ingredients.

4 Pressing firmly all over with pastry blender, cut butter into dry ingredients until mixture looks coarse and crumbly. Add currants and toss with fork to mix.

5 Pour buttermilk all over dry ingredients. With fork, toss together until soft, shaggy, slightly sticky dough forms. Dust your hand lightly with flour, then press dough into ball right in bowl.

6 Dust counter lightly with flour. Using rubber spatula, scrape dough out onto counter. Dust your hand with flour again, then pat out dough into circle about 3/4 inch (2 cm) thick.

Dip cutter into flour; place at edge of dough. Press down to cut out scone. Lift onto baking sheet.

7 Cut scones as close as possible to each other. Press scraps together and cut more scones. Gather up any bits of dough and press into one last scone — the cook's scone!

8 Break egg into bowl; with fork, beat until yolk and white are blended. With pastry brush, brush egg over top of each scone.

9 Bake on baking sheet for 12 to 15 minutes or until scones are golden and puffed. Wearing oven mitts, remove baking sheet from oven; lift off scones and let cool on rack if not eating immediately.

Makes 12 scones.

## VARIATION

● DRIED FRUIT AND LEMON SCONES: Substitute 1/2 cup (125 mL) raisins, dried blueberries, dried cranberries, chopped dried cherries (not glacé), apricots or prunes for currants. Add 2 tsp (10 mL) grated lemon rind to dry mixture.

Budding bakers are sure to get raves when they serve scones hot from the oven.

### EQUIPMENT LIST
- baking sheet
- dry measuring cups
- measuring spoons
- large bowl
- whisk
- small knife
- cutting board
- pastry blender
- liquid measuring cup
- 2-1/2-inch (6 cm) cookie cutter
- lifter
- small bowl
- fork
- pastry brush
- oven mitts
- wire rack

# Applesauce Bran Muffins ▼

Make your own applesauce (recipe, p. 27) or put it on the shopping list so you can make these moist, healthy snacks. Wrapped and frozen, big muffins like these make excellent quickie breakfasts and tuck very nicely into lunch bags.

### EQUIPMENT LIST

- pastry brush or paper muffin cups
- 2 large bowls
- whisk
- liquid measuring cup
- measuring spoons
- wooden spoons
- rubber spatula
- muffin pans for 12 muffins
- ice cream scoop or large spoon
- oven mitts
- wire rack
- table knife

| 1 | egg | 1 |
|---|---|---|
| 1 cup | applesauce | 250 mL |
| 2/3 cup | buttermilk | 150 mL |
| 1/3 cup | packed brown sugar | 75 mL |
| 1/4 cup | fancy molasses | 50 mL |
| 1/4 cup | vegetable oil | 50 mL |
| 1 tsp | vanilla | 5 mL |
| 1 cup | natural wheat bran | 250 mL |
| 2 cups | all-purpose flour | 500 mL |
| 1 tsp | baking soda | 5 mL |
| 1 tsp | cinnamon | 5 mL |
| 1 tsp | salt | 5 mL |
| 1 cup | raisins | 250 mL |

1 Place oven rack in center of oven; turn on heat to 375°F (190°C). Brush each muffin cup lightly with oil or line with paper liner; set aside.

2 Break egg into large bowl. Measure applesauce, buttermilk, brown sugar, molasses, oil and vanilla into same bowl. Whisk together with egg until smooth.

3 Add bran; with wooden spoon, stir well. Set aside for 5 minutes for bran to soften and absorb some of the liquid.

4 Measure flour, baking soda, cinnamon and salt into separate large bowl. Scrape applesauce mixture over dry ingredients. Sprinkle with raisins; with wooden spoon, stir together until combined and no streaks of flour remain.

5 Using ice cream scoop or large spoon, fill muffin cups to the top with batter. Bake for about 25 minutes or until golden and domed and tops feel firm to the touch.

6 Wearing oven mitts, remove pans from oven to rack and let cool for 5 minutes. Lift muffins out of pans and let cool completely on rack. *(Muffins can be wrapped individually in plastic wrap, enclosed in an airtight container or large freezer bag and frozen for up to 2 weeks.)*

Makes 12 muffins.

**TIP:** Let wrapped and frozen muffin stand at room temperature for 2 hours before eating. Or unwrap muffin, re-wrap in paper towel and microwave at High for 30 seconds.

# Anything-Goes Muffins

| 2 cups | all-purpose flour | 500 mL |
|---|---|---|
| 3/4 cup | packed brown sugar | 175 mL |
| 2 tsp | baking powder | 10 mL |
| 1/2 tsp | baking soda | 2 mL |
| 1/2 tsp | cinnamon | 2 mL |
| 1/4 tsp | salt | 1 mL |
| 2 | eggs | 2 |
| 1 cup | milk | 250 mL |
| 1/4 cup | vegetable oil | 50 mL |
| 1 tsp | grated orange rind | 5 mL |
| 1 tsp | vanilla | 5 mL |
| 1 cup | fresh blueberries | 250 mL |

1 Place oven rack in center of oven; turn on heat to 375°F (190°C). Line each muffin cup with paper liner; set aside.

2 Measure flour, sugar, baking powder, baking soda, cinnamon and salt into large bowl. With your fingers, break brown sugar apart until no lumps remain. Whisk to blend ingredients together.

3 Break eggs into medium bowl; add milk, oil, orange rind and vanilla. Whisk until smooth and no streaks remain. With rubber spatula, scrape over dry ingredients.

4 Sprinkle with blueberries. With wooden spoon, stir together just until only a few streaks of flour remain.

5 Using ice cream scoop, fill muffin cups almost full with batter.

6 Bake for 20 to 25 minutes or until golden and domed. Wearing oven mitts, remove pans from oven to rack and let cool for 10 minutes. Lift muffins out of pans and let cool completely on rack.

Makes 12 muffins.

With this recipe, you can add in to your heart's content — fresh blueberries, currants, raspberries, raisins or chocolate chips.

**EQUIPMENT LIST**
- muffin pans for 12 muffins
- paper muffin cups
- dry measuring cups
- measuring spoons
- large bowl
- whisk
- medium bowl
- liquid measuring cup
- cheese grater
- wooden spoon
- rubber spatula
- ice cream scoop or large spoon
- oven mitts
- wire rack

# Carrot Orange Muffin Bars

| 1 cup | all-purpose flour | 250 mL |
|---|---|---|
| 1/2 cup | whole wheat flour | 125 mL |
| 1 tsp | baking powder | 5 mL |
| 1 tsp | cinnamon | 5 mL |
| 1 tsp | grated orange rind | 5 mL |
| 1/2 tsp | baking soda | 2 mL |
| 1/2 tsp | salt | 2 mL |
| 1/2 cup | raisins | 125 mL |
| 1 | egg | 1 |
| 1/2 cup | packed brown sugar | 125 mL |
| 1/3 cup | orange juice | 75 mL |
| 1/4 cup | vegetable oil | 50 mL |
| 1 tsp | vanilla | 5 mL |
| 1-1/2 cups | grated carrots | 375 mL |

1 Place oven rack in center of oven; turn on heat to 350°F (180°C). With pastry brush, lightly brush cake pan with oil; set aside.

2 Measure all-purpose and whole wheat flours, baking powder, cinnamon, orange rind, baking soda and salt into large bowl. Whisk to blend ingredients together. Sprinkle with raisins.

3 Break egg into medium bowl; add brown sugar, orange juice, oil and vanilla. Whisk until smooth and no streaks remain. Stir in carrots.

4 With rubber spatula, scrape over dry ingredients. With wooden spoon, stir together just until only a few streaks of flour remain. Scrape into pan; smooth top.

5 Bake for 30 to 35 minutes or until golden and cake tester inserted in center comes out clean. Wearing oven mitts, remove pan from oven and let cool on rack. Cut into bars.

Makes 12 bars.

Take some muffin batter, bake it in a cake pan — and you've got a snacking-style muffin cake you can cut into bars.

**EQUIPMENT LIST**
- pastry brush
- 9-inch (2.5 L) square cake pan
- dry measuring cups
- measuring spoons
- large bowl
- whisk
- fork
- medium bowl
- liquid measuring cup
- cheese grater
- wooden spoon
- rubber spatula
- ice cream scoop or large spoon
- oven mitts
- wire rack

# Chocolate Chip Cookies ▼

What's the secret to great chocolate chip cookies? Lots of chips, of course, and a very generous splash of real, not artificial, vanilla extract.

**EQUIPMENT LIST**
• pastry brush
• 2 rimless baking sheets
• table knife
• dry measuring cups
• large bowl
• electric mixer
• small bowl
• medium bowl
• measuring spoons
• whisk
• cutting board
• sharp knife
• wooden spoon
• teaspoon
• fork
• oven mitts
• lifter
• wire rack

| | | |
|---|---|---|
| 1/2 cup | butter | 125 mL |
| 1/2 cup | shortening | 125 mL |
| 1 cup | granulated sugar | 250 mL |
| 1/2 cup | packed brown sugar | 125 mL |
| 2 | eggs | 2 |
| 2 tsp | vanilla | 10 mL |
| 2 cups | all-purpose flour | 500 mL |
| 1 tsp | baking soda | 5 mL |
| 1/2 tsp | salt | 2 mL |
| 2 cups | chocolate chips | 500 mL |
| 1 cup | chopped walnuts or pecans | 250 mL |

1 Place oven rack in center of oven; turn on heat to 375°F (190°C). With pastry brush and a little shortening, lightly grease baking sheets; set aside.

2 Measure butter and shortening into large bowl. With electric mixer, beat at high speed until fluffy and light-colored. Add granulated sugar and brown sugar, 1/2 cup (125 mL) at a time, beating well until even fluffier.

3 Break 1 of the eggs into small bowl and add to batter; beat until blended in. Break second egg into small bowl; add to batter along with vanilla and beat until smooth.

4 In medium bowl, whisk together flour, baking soda and salt. Pour over batter; with wooden spoon, mix in until no streaks of flour remain.

5 Sprinkle with chocolate chips and walnuts; stir into dough until equally distributed. Refrigerate for 20 minutes.

6 Scoop up dough by rounded teaspoonfuls (5 mL) and drop onto baking sheets, leaving 2-inch (5 cm) space between cookies. With fork, press each cookie lightly to 1/2-inch (1 cm) thickness.

7 Bake, one sheet at a time, for 8 to 12 minutes or until golden around edges and underneath. Wearing oven mitts, remove baking sheet from oven and set on rack to cool for 2 minutes.

8 Lift cookies off baking sheet and set in single layer on rack to cool completely.

9 Repeat baking with remaining baking sheet of raw cookie dough. Let first baking sheet cool completely before adding more raw dough so dough doesn't melt. Keep filling, baking and cooling cookies until all dough has been used up.

Makes about 48 cookies.

VARIATION
● REVERSE CHOCOLATE CHIP COOKIES: Replace 1/3 cup (75 mL) of the flour with unsweetened cocoa powder and use white chocolate chips or chopped white chocolate instead of dark chocolate chips.

**TIP:** Let cookies cool completely. To store, place in cookie tin, separating layers with waxed paper. Keep at room temperature for up to 5 days or freeze for up to 1 month.

# Jumbo Oatmeal Cookies

| 2/3 cup | butter, softened | 150 mL |
|---|---|---|
| 1 cup | packed brown sugar | 250 mL |
| 1 | egg | 1 |
| 1 tbsp | vanilla | 15 mL |
| 1-1/2 cups | rolled oats (not instant) | 375 mL |
| 1 cup | all-purpose flour | 250 mL |
| 1/2 tsp | baking powder | 2 mL |
| 1/2 tsp | baking soda | 2 mL |
| 1/2 tsp | cinnamon | 2 mL |
| 1/4 tsp | salt | 1 mL |

1 Place oven rack in center of oven; turn on heat to 350°F (180°C). With pastry brush and a little shortening, lightly grease baking sheets; set aside.

2 Measure butter into large bowl. With electric mixer, beat at high speed until fluffy and light-colored. Add sugar; beat until batter is even fluffier.

3 Break egg into small bowl and add to batter along with vanilla. Beat until smooth.

4 In medium bowl, whisk together rolled oats, flour, baking powder, baking soda, cinnamon and salt. Pour over batter; with wooden spoon, mix in until no streaks of flour remain. Refrigerate for 30 minutes or cover top with plastic wrap and store for up to 1 day.

5 Scoop up dough by rounded tablespoonfuls (15 mL) and roll quickly between palms into balls. Place on baking sheets, leaving 2-inch (5 cm) space between cookies.

6 Bake, one sheet at a time, for 12 to 15 minutes or until golden around edges and underneath but still slightly soft in center. Wearing oven mitts, remove baking sheet from oven. Lift cookies off baking sheet and set in single layer on rack to cool completely.

7 Repeat baking with remaining baking sheet of raw cookie dough. Let first baking sheet cool completely before adding more raw dough so dough doesn't melt. Keep filling, baking and cooling cookies until all dough has been used up.

Makes about 24 cookies.

**TIP:** For 48 smaller cookies, use heaping teaspoonfuls (5 mL) of dough to make balls. Bake for 8 to 12 minutes.

Think of oatmeal cookies as your big chance to be creative! You can add up to 1 cup (250 mL) of delicious stuff such as raisins, currants, dried cranberries or cherries, snipped apricots, chopped dates, mixed chopped dried fruit and chopped pecans or walnuts. Or go crazy with chocolate chips or colored candy-coated chocolate.

**EQUIPMENT LIST**
- pastry brush
- 2 rimless baking sheets
- table knife
- dry measuring cups
- large bowl
- electric mixer
- measuring spoons
- small bowl
- medium bowl
- whisk
- wooden spoon
- fork
- oven mitts
- lifter
- wire rack

## TIPS FOR BAKERS

- Choose large bowls when baking. The size helps keep ingredients in the bowl, not splashed onto the counter or floor.
- Never measure out ingredients over the batter bowl in case of a spill.
- When beating egg whites or cream, choose a bowl with straight sides so that the beaters reach as much of the liquid as possible with each turn.

# Whole Wheat Peanut Butter Cookies ▼

Some old-fashioned cookies never go out of style. Here's one to fill your cookie jar.

### EQUIPMENT LIST

- pastry brush
- 2 rimless baking sheets
- table knife
- dry measuring cups
- large bowl
- electric mixer
- measuring spoons
- small bowl
- medium bowl
- whisk
- wooden spoon
- fork
- oven mitts
- lifter
- wire rack

| | | |
|---|---|---|
| 3/4 cup | chunky peanut butter | 175 mL |
| 3/4 cup | liquid honey | 175 mL |
| 1/2 cup | granulated sugar | 125 mL |
| 1/3 cup | butter, softened | 75 mL |
| 2 tsp | vanilla | 10 mL |
| 2 | eggs | 2 |
| 3 cups | whole wheat flour | 750 mL |
| 1 tsp | baking soda | 5 mL |
| 1/2 tsp | salt | 2 mL |

1 Place oven rack in center of oven; turn on heat to 375°F (190°C). With pastry brush and a little shortening, lightly grease baking sheets; set aside.

2 Measure peanut butter, honey, granulated sugar and butter into large bowl. With electric mixer, beat at high speed until fluffy and light-colored. Beat in vanilla.

3 Break 1 of the eggs into small bowl and add to batter; beat until blended in. Break second egg into small bowl; add to batter and beat well.

4 In medium bowl, whisk together flour, baking soda and salt. Pour over batter; with wooden spoon, mix in until no streaks of flour remain.

5 Scoop up dough by rounded tablespoonfuls (15 mL) and drop onto baking sheets, leaving 1-inch (2.5 cm) space between cookies. With fork, press each cookie lightly to make crisscross pattern and flatten cookies to 1/2-inch (1 cm) thickness.

6 Bake, one sheet at a time, for 10 minutes or until firm and slightly darkened around edges and underneath. Wearing oven mitts, remove baking sheet from oven and set on rack to cool for 2 minutes.

7 Lift cookies off baking sheet and set in single layer on rack to cool completely.

8 Repeat baking with remaining baking sheet of raw cookie dough. Let first baking sheet cool completely before adding more raw dough so dough doesn't melt. Keep filling, baking and cooling cookies until all dough has been used up.

Makes about 48 cookies.

### VARIATION

● PEANUTTY PEANUT BUTTER COOKIES: You can stir in up to 3/4 cup (175 mL) chopped unsalted peanuts to dough after blending in flour mixture.

# Chocolate Fudge Brownies

| | | |
|---|---|---|
| 5 oz | semisweet chocolate | 150 g |
| 1/3 cup | butter | 75 mL |
| 3/4 cup | granulated sugar | 175 mL |
| 2 tsp | vanilla | 10 mL |
| 2 | eggs | 2 |
| 1/2 cup | all-purpose flour | 125 mL |
| Pinch | salt | Pinch |
| 1/2 cup | semisweet chocolate chips | 125 mL |
| 1 tsp | (approx) icing sugar | 5 mL |

1 Place oven rack in center of oven; turn on heat to 350°F (180°C). With pastry brush and a little shortening, lightly grease cake pan; set aside.

2 Place chocolate on cutting board; with sharp knife, chop coarsely. Drop chocolate and butter into saucepan; place over medium-low heat. Melt, stirring occasionally, until smooth.

3 Remove chocolate mixture from heat and let cool for 5 minutes. Whisk in sugar and vanilla.

4 Break 1 of the eggs into small bowl and add to chocolate mixture; whisk until blended in. Break second egg into small bowl; add to mixture and whisk well.

5 Add half of the flour; with wooden spoon, stir until blended. Add remaining flour and salt; stir until no streaks of flour remain.

6 Sprinkle with chocolate chips; stir until evenly distributed. With rubber spatula, scrape into pan and smooth top. Bake for 25 to 30 minutes.

7 Stick cake tester into center of brownies. If it comes out clean with just a few small crumbs clinging to it, brownies are done. If not, bake a few minutes longer. Wearing oven mitts, remove pan from oven and let cool completely on rack.

8 Hold sieve over brownies; spoon in icing sugar. Tapping edge of sieve lightly, move sieve over brownies until surface is dusted lightly, adding more sugar as needed.

9 With sharp knife, cut brownies into squares. Cover with plastic wrap if storing for a day to two.

Makes 20 brownies.

## VARIATIONS

● NUTTY CHOCOLATE BROWNIES: Spread 3/4 cup (175 mL) chopped pecans or walnuts onto baking sheet. Toast in 350°F (180°C) oven for 6 minutes or until fragrant and slightly darker in color. Let cool completely and add to brownies instead of chocolate chips.

● CHOCOLATE FRUIT BROWNIES: Substitute dried cranberries, dried strawberries, dried cherries or chopped dried apricots for chocolate chips.

● CHOCOLATE TOFFEE BROWNIES: Add 1/2 cup (125 mL) toffee bits to batter along with chocolate chips.

Brownies are hard to resist when they're dark, dense and packed with chocolate chips. They also make great party food and are an excellent offering for a bake sale. Try the master recipe, then discover how toasted nuts, toffee bits and dried fruit such as cherries give brownies a whole new meaning.

**EQUIPMENT LIST**
- pastry brush
- 8-inch (2 L) square cake pan
- sharp knife
- cutting board
- medium heavy saucepan
- wooden spoon
- rubber spatula
- dry measuring cups
- measuring spoons
- whisk
- small bowl
- oven mitts
- cake tester
- wire rack
- spoon
- small fine sieve

# Black and Orange Nanaimo Bars

Nanaimo bars are easy to make in stages and are always a hit at school bake sales or parties. Why not make these for Halloween?

**EQUIPMENT LIST**

- dry measuring cups
- medium heavy saucepan
- wooden spoon
- medium bowl
- whisk
- oven mitts
- rubber spatula
- cheese grater
- 9-inch (2.5 L) square cake pan
- electric mixer
- measuring spoons
- cutting board
- sharp knife
- small heavy saucepan

| | | |
|---|---|---|
| 1/2 cup | butter | 125 mL |
| 1/3 cup | unsweetened cocoa powder | 75 mL |
| 1/4 cup | granulated sugar | 50 mL |
| 1 | egg | 1 |
| 1-3/4 cups | graham cracker crumbs | 425 mL |
| 1/2 cup | finely chopped nuts | 125 mL |
| 1/2 cup | shredded coconut | 125 mL |
| 1 tsp | grated orange rind | 5 mL |
| | **MIDDLE LAYER** | |
| 1/2 cup | butter | 125 mL |
| 2 tbsp | custard powder | 25 mL |
| 2 tbsp | frozen orange juice concentrate, thawed | 25 mL |
| 1 tsp | grated orange rind | 5 mL |
| 2 cups | icing sugar | 500 mL |
| | Orange food coloring (optional) | |
| | **TOP LAYER** | |
| 4 oz | semisweet chocolate | 125 g |
| 2 tbsp | butter | 25 mL |

1 Measure butter, cocoa and sugar into saucepan. Place over medium heat; cook, stirring occasionally, until butter melts and sugar dissolves.

2 Break egg into bowl; whisk to blend yolk and white. Wearing oven mitts and whisking constantly, pour butter mixture over egg. With rubber spatula, scrape back into saucepan.

3 Return saucepan to heat; cook, stirring, for 2 minutes or until egg mixture is thickened and smooth. Remove from heat.

4 Add crumbs, nuts, coconut and orange rind; stir to blend well. With spatula, scrape into cake pan and spread evenly; press evenly with fingertips. Refrigerate for 30 minutes.

5 MIDDLE LAYER: Meanwhile, measure butter into bowl and let soften. With electric mixer, beat in custard powder, orange juice concentrate and orange rind. At low speed, beat in icing sugar, 1/2 cup (125 mL) at a time, and coloring (if using). Spread over base; refrigerate for about 1 hour or until set.

6 TOP LAYER: Place chocolate on cutting board; with sharp knife, chop coarsely. Transfer to small saucepan and add butter; heat over low heat, stirring often with wooden spoon, until melted and smooth. Pour over middle layer, spreading evenly. Return to refrigerator for about 30 minutes or until firm.

7 Cover with plastic wrap and store in refrigerator. With sharp knife, cut into bars to serve.

Makes 25 bars.

## GREASING PANS

*Here are three different ways to grease cake or muffin pans or baking sheets before baking. Be sure to check the recipe first, to see which method is specified.*

- Use a pastry brush and a few drops of vegetable oil to coat the whole cake pan, especially the corners; muffins cups; or the entire surface of a baking sheet.
- Or, brush on light coating of shortening.
- Or, spray with oil baking spray.

# Confetti Chocolate Bark

| | | |
|---|---|---|
| 1 lb | semisweet or milk chocolate | 500 g |
| 1-1/2 cups | candy-coated chocolate pieces | 375 mL |

1 Line baking sheet with foil; set aside. On cutting board and using sharp knife, chop chocolate coarsely. Dump into bowl; set aside.

2 Pour about 2 inches (5 cm) water into saucepan; bring to boil over high heat. Reduce heat to low. Carefully place bowl over hot water. Melt chocolate, stirring often, until smooth.

3 Wearing oven mitts, carefully remove bowl from heat. With wooden spoon, stir in candy-coated chocolate pieces.

4 Pour chocolate mixture onto baking sheet; with rubber spatula, spread into rectangle about 1/2 inch (1 cm) thick.

5 Refrigerate for at least 1 hour or until hardened. Break into pieces.

Makes about 1-1/2 lb (750 g) candy, or 32 pieces.

### VARIATIONS

● FRUIT AND NUT BARK: You can add 1-1/2 cups (375 mL) of your favorite nuts and fruit instead of the candy-coated chocolate. Slivered almonds, chopped pecans, walnuts or hazelnuts, dried cherries, cranberries, snipped apricots and raisins are some suggestions. If you toast the nuts (see p. 69), they are even more delicious.

● COOKIES AND CREAM CHOCOLATE BARK: Substitute white chocolate for semisweet. Substitute about 12 cream-filled chocolate cookies for candy-coated chocolate, chopped with sharp knife to make 1-1/2 cups (375 mL).

Here's a great gift idea for any time of the year.

**EQUIPMENT LIST**
- rimmed baking sheet
- aluminum foil
- sharp knife
- cutting board
- heatproof medium bowl
- medium saucepan
- oven mitts
- wooden spoon
- dry measuring cups
- rubber spatula

# Hello Dolly Bars

| | | |
|---|---|---|
| 1/2 cup | (approx) butter | 125 mL |
| 2 cups | graham cracker crumbs | 500 mL |
| 1 cup | semisweet chocolate chips | 250 mL |
| 1 cup | butterscotch chips | 250 mL |
| 1-1/2 cups | chopped pecans | 375 mL |
| 1 cup | unsweetened shredded or desiccated coconut | 250 mL |
| 1 | can (300 mL) sweetened condensed milk | 1 |

1 Place oven rack in center of oven; turn on heat to 350°F (180°C). With a little of the butter and using fingers, lightly grease baking dish; set aside.

2 Measure graham cracker crumbs into bowl. Measure remaining butter into saucepan. Place over medium heat, stirring with wooden spoon until melted. Pour over crumbs; toss until crumbs are evenly moistened.

3 Scrape crumb mixture into baking dish; with fingers, pat into even layer. Scatter chocolate and butterscotch chips evenly over crumbs. Sprinkle with pecans, then coconut. Drizzle condensed milk evenly over top.

4 Bake for about 30 minutes or until golden. Wearing oven mitts, remove baking dish from oven and let cool on rack. With sharp knife, cut into squares.

Makes 30 squares.

These bars are ultra-rich, so cut them into small pieces for a party.

**EQUIPMENT LIST**
- 13- x 9-inch (3 L) glass baking dish or (3.5 L) cake pan
- dry measuring cups
- large bowl
- small heavy saucepan
- wooden spoon
- rubber spatula
- can opener
- oven mitts
- wire rack

# No-Bake Crispy Rice Fruit Balls

Fruit — lots of it — delivers a double hit of sweetness and flavor in these easy-to-make treats.

**EQUIPMENT LIST**
- cutting board
- sharp knife
- dry measuring cups
- food processor
- rubber spatula
- measuring spoons
- wide shallow dish
- waxed paper
- shallow cookie container

| | | |
|---|---|---|
| 1/2 cup | dried figs | 125 mL |
| 1/2 cup | toasted whole almonds | 125 mL |
| 1/2 cup | raisins | 125 mL |
| 1/2 cup | dried apples | 125 mL |
| 1/2 cup | pitted dates | 125 mL |
| 2 tbsp | orange juice | 25 mL |
| 3/4 cup | crispy rice cereal | 175 mL |

1 Place figs on cutting board; with sharp knife, cut off hard tips. Drop figs, almonds, raisins, apples and dates into food processor work bowl. Fasten lid and whirl until fruit and nuts are chopped.

2 Stop the processor and use spatula to scrape down side of bowl. Whirl again until paste forms.

3 Add orange juice; whirl until blended into paste. Carefully remove blade from work bowl; scrape off paste and return paste to bowl.

4 Spread cereal in shallow bowl. Scoop up paste by rounded teaspoonfuls (5 mL) and roll between palms into balls. Roll in cereal to coat all over. Arrange on waxed paper in cookie container.

Makes 24 balls.

# Crunchy Cereal Squares

Sweet, yes — but seeds, dried fruit and nuts rev up the food value in these tasty squares.

**EQUIPMENT LIST**
- 13- x 9-inch (3.5 L) cake pan
- aluminum foil
- pastry brush
- dry measuring cups
- plastic storage bag
- large metal bowl
- cutting board
- sharp knife
- wooden spoon
- liquid measuring cup
- small saucepan
- oven mitts
- rubber spatula
- table knife
- wire rack

| | | |
|---|---|---|
| 4 cups | corn flakes | 1 L |
| 1 cup | shredded unsweetened coconut | 250 mL |
| 1/2 cup | sunflower seeds | 125 mL |
| 1/2 cup | toasted almonds, coarsely chopped | 125 mL |
| 1/2 cup | dried apricots, chopped | 125 mL |
| 1/2 cup | pitted dates, coarsely chopped | 125 mL |
| 1/2 cup | corn syrup | 125 mL |
| 1/4 cup | butter | 50 mL |
| 1/4 cup | water | 50 mL |
| 1/2 cup | packed brown sugar | 125 mL |

1 Place oven rack in center of oven; turn on heat to 325°F (160°C). Line cake pan with foil; with pastry brush, brush foil lightly with butter. Set aside.

2 Measure corn flakes into plastic bag; lay on counter and crush lightly with hands. Dump corn flakes into bowl along with coconut, sunflower seeds, almonds, apricots and dates. With spoon, toss to mix.

3 Measure corn syrup, butter and water into saucepan. Place over medium heat; cook, stirring occasionally with wooden spoon, until butter melts.

4 Add sugar; stir until dissolved. Increase heat to medium-high; bring to full rolling boil. Boil, without stirring, for 3 minutes.

5 Wearing oven mitts, carefully pour syrup over cornflake mixture. Immediately start tossing with wooden spoon to coat cereal, fruit, seeds and nuts evenly.

6 Scoop out into cake pan; spread evenly and press firmly. Bake for 30 minutes.

7 Wearing oven mitts, transfer pan from oven to rack. Run knife around inside edge of pan to release cereal block. Let cool completely.

8 Turn pan over onto cutting board; peel off foil. With sharp knife, cut into squares.

Makes 20 squares.

# Butterscotch Crunch Bars

| | | |
|---|---|---|
| 1 cup | (approx) unsalted butter | 250 mL |
| 28 | graham crackers | 28 |
| 1 cup | packed brown sugar | 250 mL |
| 1-1/2 cups | toasted sliced almonds | 375 mL |

1 Place oven rack in center of oven; turn on heat to 375°F (190°C). With a little of the butter and using fingers, lightly grease jelly roll pan. Place graham crackers in single layer in pan; set aside.

2 Measure remaining butter into saucepan; place over medium heat to melt, stirring often. Add sugar; whisk until combined but do not bring to boil.

3 Remove from heat; stir in almonds. Spread almond mixture over crackers. Bake for 10 minutes or until bubbling.

4 Wearing oven mitts, remove pan from oven and place on rack. Let cool for 10 minutes. With sharp knife, cut into bars.

Makes 28 bars.

C risp and chewy, these bars start out with graham crackers.

**EQUIPMENT LIST**
- 15- x 10-inch (40 x 25 cm) jelly roll pan
- sharp knife
- dry measuring cups
- medium heavy saucepan
- whisk
- wooden spoon
- oven mitts
- wire rack

# Peanut Butter S'mores

| | | |
|---|---|---|
| | Peanut butter | |
| 8 | graham crackers | 8 |
| | Chocolate chips | |
| 2 | marshmallows | 2 |

1 Spread peanut butter thinly over 4 of the graham crackers. Sprinkle lightly with chocolate chips. Place these crackers on plate.

2 Snip marshmallows in half; place, cut side down, on chocolate chips.

3 Microwave at High for about 20 seconds or until marshmallows are soft and chocolate has melted. Top with remaining crackers and serve warm.

Makes 4 servings.

T he microwave oven invites you to make this summer-camp treat anytime at home.

**EQUIPMENT LIST**
- table knife
- microwaveable plate
- scissors
- oven mitts

## TOASTING NUTS

*Almost all nuts taste nuttier and are more delicious if toasted. Here's how.*

● If you are baking and have the oven on, toast nuts on baking sheet at 350°F (180°C) for 5 to 8 minutes or until fragrant and slightly darkened. Watch carefully and stir nuts at least once during the toasting time, as the ones around the edge of the pan tend to brown more quickly than the ones in the center.

● Chopped nuts brown faster than whole nuts, so cut back the time to 2 to 4 minutes.

● You can also toasts seeds this way and for the same length of time as chopped nuts.

● Here are three different ways to toast nuts without turning on the oven.

1 For small amounts, place on tray in toaster oven and toast at 350°F (180°C) for 5 to 8 minutes.

2 Place in small skillet and heat over medium heat, stirring nuts often, for about 8 minutes.

3 Spread on microwaveable plate and microwave at High for 5 to 8 minutes, stirring once or twice.

# Let's Do It Together

Double the fun in the kitchen by inviting your family or a favorite grownup to help you make these awesome holiday and birthday projects.

## Sugar Cookies ▶

With this easy-roll cookie dough, you can choose the shapes to suit the occasion — bunnies or ducks for Easter, stars and Santas for Christmas or ghosts and witches for Halloween. Adults may have to roll out the dough, but kids can help cut out shapes and take charge of the icing and sprinkles.

**EQUIPMENT LIST**
- rimless baking sheets
- parchment paper
- dry measuring cups
- liquid measuring cup
- measuring spoons
- small bowl
- medium bowl
- large bowl
- electric mixer
- wooden spoon
- plastic wrap
- rolling pin
- cookie cutters
- wire racks

| | | |
|---|---|---|
| 1 cup | butter, softened | 250 mL |
| 1 cup | packed brown sugar | 250 mL |
| 1 | egg | 1 |
| 1 tsp | vanilla | 5 mL |
| 2 cups | all-purpose flour | 500 mL |
| 1/2 tsp | baking powder | 2 mL |
| 1/4 tsp | nutmeg | 1 mL |
| Pinch | salt | Pinch |
| | ICING | |
| 2-3/4 cups | icing sugar | 675 mL |
| 2 | egg whites | 2 |
| | Food coloring | |

1 Line baking sheets with parchment paper or leave ungreased; set aside.

2 In bowl, beat butter until light and fluffy; gradually beat in brown sugar. Beat in egg and vanilla. In separate bowl, stir together flour, baking powder, nutmeg and salt; using wooden spoon, stir into butter mixture.

3 Divide dough into quarters; flatten slightly. Wrap each in plastic wrap and refrigerate for at least 1 hour or for up to 24 hours.

4 On lightly floured surface, roll out each portion of dough to 1/4-inch (5 mm) thickness. Using cookie cutters, cut out shapes; carefully place, 1 inch (2.5 cm) apart, on baking sheets.

5 Bake in 375°F (190°C) oven for 10 to 12 minutes or until light golden on bottom and edges. Let cool for 1 minute on baking sheets; transfer to racks. Let cool completely.

6 ICING: In bowl, beat icing sugar with egg whites until thick and smooth. Divide among small bowls; stir in food coloring. Decorate cookies as desired.

Makes about 36 cookies.

**TIPS**
- For the most vivid colored icing, use food coloring paste instead of liquid drops.
- To prevent dough from sticking to rolling pin and counter, roll out between sheets of waxed paper or on pastry cloth with stockinette-covered rolling pin.

# Dino Cake ◄

| | | |
|---|---|---|
| 2 cups | boiling water | 500 mL |
| 1 cup | unsweetened cocoa powder | 250 mL |
| 1 cup | butter, softened | 250 mL |
| 2 cups | granulated sugar | 500 mL |
| 4 | eggs | 4 |
| 1 tbsp | vanilla | 15 mL |
| 2-3/4 cups | all-purpose flour | 675 mL |
| 1-1/2 tsp | baking soda | 7 mL |
| 1/2 tsp | each baking powder and salt | 2 mL |
| 30 | gumdrop leaves | 30 |
| | Assorted candies | |
| | **ICING** | |
| 1-1/4 cups | butter, softened | 300 mL |
| 5-3/4 cups | icing sugar | 1.425 L |
| 1/2 cup | whipping cream | 125 mL |
| | Purple and green food coloring | |

**1** Grease cake pans; line bottoms with waxed or parchment paper. Set aside.

**2** In small bowl, whisk water with cocoa until smooth; let cool to room temperature. In large bowl and using electric mixer, beat butter with sugar just until blended; beat in eggs, two at a time, and vanilla.

**3** Stir together flour, baking soda, baking powder and salt. Stir into butter mixture alternately with liquid, making three additions of flour and two of liquid. Pour into prepared pans.

**4** Bake in 350°F (180°C) oven for 30 to 40 minutes or until cakes spring back when lightly touched. Let cool in pan on rack for 20 minutes. Invert onto baking sheet, then invert onto rack; let cool. Peel off paper.

**5** ICING: In bowl, beat butter until light. Alternately beat in sugar and cream, making three additions of sugar and two of cream. Transfer 1/2 cup (125 mL) to small bowl; tint purple with food coloring. Tint remaining icing green.

**6** With serrated knife, cut 1 of the cakes as shown. With knife, cut horizontally through both A pieces to form 4 legs.

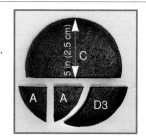

**7** Cut remaining cake as shown. Turn 1 of the C pieces over; spread thinly with green icing. Top with remaining C piece. Stand, cut side down, on cake board to form body; cut off corner of 1 side diagonally to form chest.

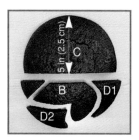

**8** Arrange pieces D1, D2 and D3 as shown to form tail, attaching together with icing. Trim to shape of tail, discarding scraps.

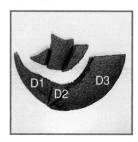

**9** Attach tail to body with icing. Cover belly and chest with purple icing. Cover tail and remaining body with green icing. Spread edge of each leg with icing; press to side of body. Cover outside of legs with icing.

**10** Spread icing over front and back of head piece (B). Attach to body with four 6-inch (15 cm) skewers, inserting 2 through lower neck and 2 through head as shown. Spread sides with icing.

**11** Halve gumdrop leaves to form 2 leaves; insert from top of head to tail. Attach candies for eyes, mouth and claws.

Makes 20 servings.

Invite a hip and handsome dinosaur to your party. He may look impressive but he's surprisingly easy to make — all you need are two simple 9-inch (1.5 L) round cakes, and lot's of green icing!

**EQUIPMENT LIST**
- 2 9-inch (1.5 L) round cake pans
- liquid measuring cup
- dry measuring cups
- measuring spoons
- whisk
- rubber spatula
- waxed or parchment paper
- small bowl
- medium bowl
- large bowl
- wire racks
- serrated knife
- pastry brush
- scissors
- electric mixer
- large bowl
- baking sheet
- large cake board or tray
- palette knife
- wooden skewers

# Pool Party Cake ▶

Last one into the pool! gains new meaning when birthday party guests get a look at this cake. Bulk food stores are a good place to find candies in the right amounts needed for projects such as this one.

**EQUIPMENT LIST**
- 13- x 9-inch (3.5 L) cake pan
- plastic wrap
- liquid measuring cup
- sharp knife
- spoon
- palette knife
- large cake board or tray

| | | |
|---|---|---|
| 1 | pkg (85 g) blue jelly powder | 1 |
| | White Butter Cake (recipe, p. 75) | |
| 2 cups | Basic Butter Icing (recipe, below) | 500 mL |
| 44 | multicolored cream-filled wafers | 44 |
| 1 | each piece (7 inches/18 cm long) red and green shoestring licorice | 1 |
| | Pink chocolate rounds, multicolored sprinkles and chocolate finger cookies | |
| | Doughnut-shaped jelly candies | |
| | Gum balls | |

1 Cover bottom and sides of cake pan with plastic wrap; set aside. Make jelly powder according to manufacturer's instructions but use only 3/4 cup (175 mL) cold water; pour into prepared pan. Refrigerate, uncovered, for 1 hour or until completely set.

● For easy decoration and presentation of special fantasy cakes, make a base, or cake board, by using an upside-down jelly roll pan or by covering a strong piece of cardboard with heavy-duty foil.

2 Meanwhile, cut White Butter Cake in kidney shape; place on cake board. With spoon, hollow out 1/2 inch (1 cm) from top of cake, leaving 3/4-inch (2 cm) thick walls as border. Freeze cake scraps for another use.

3 With palette knife, spread Basic Butter Icing over sides and border of cake. Trim wafers to 2-inch (5 cm) lengths or to match height of cake. Alternating colors, press wafers onto side of cake for fence, leaving 2-inch (5 cm) space uncovered for ladder.

4 With spatula, pick up long slabs of blue jelly; arrange in hollowed-out center of cake, rippling to resemble waves.

5 Cut red piece of licorice in half; arrange both halves on space on side of cake for ladder railings, pressing ends into cake to secure. Cut green licorice into small pieces for ladder steps; secure in place with icing.

6 At opposite end from ladder, press wafer in place for diving board. Around base of pool, arrange pink chocolate rounds and multicolored sprinkles for landscape. Arrange chocolate finger cookies for wooden planking.

7 Just before serving, place toy people in doughnut-shaped candy for swimmers in rafts. Add gum balls for beach balls.

Makes 16 to 20 servings.

# Basic Butter Icing

You can tint this icing or leave it plain. It's easy to spread onto a cake and just as easy to pipe for greetings.

**EQUIPMENT LIST**
- dry measuring cups
- liquid measuring cup
- bowl
- electric mixer

| | | |
|---|---|---|
| 1 cup | butter, softened | 250 mL |
| 5 cups | icing sugar | 1.25 L |
| 2/3 cup | whipping cream | 150 mL |

1 In bowl, beat butter at medium speed until light. Alternately beat in sugar and cream, making three additions of sugar and two of cream. *(Icing can be covered and refrigerated for up to 3 days; beat again before using.)*

Makes about 4 cups (1 L).

# White Butter Cake

| 4 | eggs | 4 |
|---|---|---|
| 1-1/3 cups | milk | 325 mL |
| 1 tbsp | vanilla | 15 mL |
| 4 cups | sifted cake-and-pastry flour | 1 L |
| 2 cups | granulated sugar | 500 mL |
| 5 tsp | baking powder | 25 mL |
| 1 tbsp | grated orange rind | 15 mL |
| 1 tsp | salt | 5 mL |
| 1 cup | butter, softened | 250 mL |

1 Grease bottom and sides of cake pan. Line bottom with parchment or waxed paper. Set aside.

2 In bowl, whisk together eggs, 1/3 cup (75 mL) of the milk and vanilla; set aside.

3 In large bowl, stir together flour, sugar, baking powder, orange rind and salt. Beat in butter and remaining milk at medium speed for 2 minutes or until fluffy. Beat in egg mixture in three additions, beating well and scraping down side of bowl between additions.

4 Scrape batter into prepared pan, smoothing top. Bake in 350°F (180°C) oven for 40 to 45 minutes or until golden, cake springs back when lightly touched and cake tester inserted in center comes out clean. Let cool in pan on rack for 20 minutes.

5 Run knife around edge of cake; invert onto baking sheet and peel off paper. Reinvert cake onto rack; let cool completely.

Makes 16 to 20 servings.

U se this delicious and reliable recipe as a foundation for all kinds of special-occasion cakes.

### EQUIPMENT LIST
- liquid measuring cup
- dry measuring cup
- measuring spoons
- sifter
- grater
- whisk
- 13- x 9-inch (3.5 L) cake pan
- parchment or waxed paper
- medium bowl
- large bowl
- electric mixer
- wooden spoon
- rubber spatula
- cake tester
- wire rack
- knife
- baking sheet

# Licorice Caramel Apples ▼

Once you've tasted this neat new take on caramel apples, you'll want to make this tasty treat even when Halloween's over.

## EQUIPMENT LIST
- baking sheet
- parchment paper
- dry measuring cups
- measuring spoons
- microwaveable bowls
- wooden spoon
- wooden stir sticks

| | Vegetable oil | |
| --- | --- | --- |
| 1-1/2 cups | assorted miniature candies | 375 mL |
| 3 | pkg (each 200 g) licorice toffee | 3 |
| 3 tbsp | water | 50 mL |
| 8 | McIntosh apples | 8 |
| 1/3 cup | orange candy moulding wafers | 75 mL |

1 Cover baking sheet with parchment paper or foil; brush lightly with oil. On baking sheet, evenly divide candies into 8 mounds. Set aside.

2 In microwaveable bowl, microwave licorice toffee and water, uncovered, at High for 2 minutes. Stir; microwave for 1 minute or until melted. (Alternatively, heat in top of double boiler over medium heat until melted.)

3 Insert wooden stir stick into stem end of each apple. Holding stick, dip 1 apple into hot toffee mixture, spooning over apple to cover completely and letting excess drip back into bowl.

4 Press end of apple into 1 candy mound, pushing candies into toffee to help adhere. Let stand.

5 Repeat with remaining apples, reheating toffee if beginning to thicken. Refrigerate apples for at least 1 hour or until firm or for up to 8 hours.

6 In small microwaveable bowl, microwave orange candy moulding wafers at Medium (50%) for about 2 minutes or until melted. (Alternatively, melt in top of double boiler over medium heat.) Stir until smooth.

7 Drizzle as desired over apples. Let stand for 30 minutes. *(Apples can be individually wrapped in plastic wrap and refrigerated for up to 1 day.)*

Makes 8 servings.

## COOKING WITH KIDS

Whenever you're cooking with kids, patience and organization are the keys to success. Set aside plenty of time, make sure you're well rested and have all the equipment and ingredients on hand before you start. Then, enjoy the occasion — and encourage with praise.

# Great Pumpkin Patch Cake ▼

| | | |
|---|---|---|
| 2 | double batches Wacky Cupcake Batter (recipe, p. 78) | 2 |
| 3 | batches Wacky Icing (recipe, p. 78) | 3 |
| | Orange food coloring | |
| | Green, black and orange candy moulding wafers | |
| | Shoestring licorice | |
| | FILLING | |
| 1 | pkg (8 oz/250 g) cream cheese, softened | 1 |
| 1/3 cup | icing sugar | 75 mL |
| 1 tbsp | grated orange rind | 15 mL |
| 2 tbsp | orange juice | 25 mL |

1 Bake each double batch of Wacky Cupcake Batter in greased Bundt pan in 350°F (180°C) oven for about 40 minutes or until cake springs back when lightly touched. Let cool in pan for 10 minutes; invert onto rack and let cool completely.

2 FILLING: In bowl, beat cream cheese; beat in icing sugar and orange rind and juice.

3 Level off base of each cake. Place one cake, rounded side down, on flat cake plate. Spread with filling; top with second cake, rounded side up, aligning ridges. Tint Wacky Icing orange; spread over cake.

4 In 250°F (120°C) oven, warm large green candle for about 5 minutes or until able to bend slightly. Insert in top of cake for stem.

5 In separate saucepans, melt each color of moulding wafers. Spoon, side by side, onto parchment paper-lined baking sheet; swirl together for marble effect. Refrigerate for at least 2 minutes or until hardened.

6 Carve as desired to resemble jack-o'-lantern eyes and mouth. Press into icing. Attach strands of licorice for eyebrows.

Makes 24 servings.

This beautiful pumpkin is made with two double batches of Wacky Cupcake Batter (see Wacky Witch Cupcakes, next page). Bake each double batch in a Bundt pan. One cake forms the bottom of the jack-o'-latern, and the second forms the top. Once aligned, the ridges are just like those of a pumpkin.

**EQUIPMENT LIST**
- dry measuring cups
- measuring spoons
- grater
- 10-inch (3 L) Bundt pan
- rubber spatula
- wire rack
- bowl
- electric mixer
  - serrated knife
  - palette knife
- flat cake plate
- 3 saucepans
- parchment paper
- baking sheet
- knife

# Wacky Witch Cupcakes ▼

For our photograph, we made the witches' hats out of regular ice cream cones dipped first in melted Oetker Chocofix (frosting mix), then in sprinkles.

**EQUIPMENT LIST**
- dry measuring cups
- measuring spoons
- liquid measuring cup
- sifter
- large bowl
- medium bowl
- wooden spoon
- paper muffin cups
- muffin pans for 10 cupcakes
- wire rack
- electric mixer
- palette knife

| | | |
|---|---|---|
| 10 | Oreo cookie-flavored ice-cream cones | 10 |
| | Orange and black candy sprinkles | |
| 20 | licorice allsorts | 20 |
| 10 | each gumdrop crescents, unshelled peanuts and miniature candies | 10 |
| | Shoestring licorice | |
| | **WACKY CUPCAKE BATTER** | |
| 1-1/4 cups | all-purpose flour | 300 mL |
| 3/4 cup | granulated sugar | 175 mL |
| 1/2 cup | unsweetened cocoa powder, sifted | 125 mL |
| 1 tsp | each baking powder and baking soda | 5 mL |
| 1/2 tsp | salt | 2 mL |
| 1/4 cup | vegetable oil | 50 mL |
| 1 | egg | 1 |
| 1 tbsp | white vinegar | 15 mL |
| 3/4 cup | water | 175 mL |
| | **WACKY ICING** | |
| 1/4 cup | butter, softened | 50 mL |
| 2 cups | icing sugar | 500 mL |
| 1 tbsp | whipping cream | 15 mL |
| | Green and yellow food coloring | |

1 WACKY CUPCAKE BATTER: In large bowl, stir together flour, sugar, cocoa, baking powder, baking soda and salt. Make three hollows in mixture. Pour oil into first hollow, egg into second and vinegar into third. Pour water over top; mix until smooth.

2 Spoon into 10 greased or paper-lined muffin cups. Bake in 350°F (180°C) oven for 15 to 20 minutes or until tops spring back when lightly touched. Transfer to rack and let cool completely.

3 WACKY ICING: Meanwhile, in bowl, beat butter with sugar until smooth. Beat in cream. Using green and yellow food coloring, tint pale green. Reserving 1/4 cup (50 mL), spread over cupcakes.

4 Using most of the remaining icing, coat wide end of cones; dip into sprinkles. Attach 1 cone to each cupcake to resemble hat.

5 Decorate with allsorts for eyes, gumdrop for mouth and peanut for nose. Using frosting, attach miniature candy to nose for wart. Add licorice for hair.

Makes 10 cupcakes.

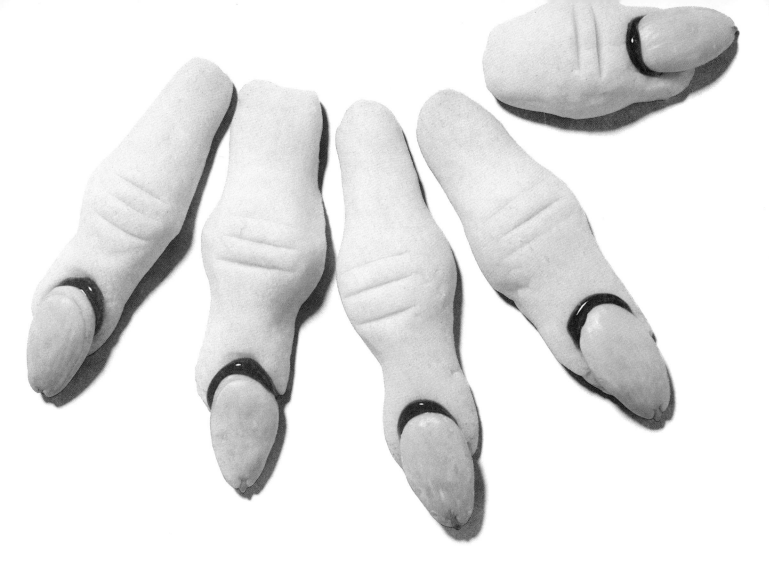

# Edible Creepy Witch's Fingers ▲

| | | |
|---|---|---|
| 1 cup | butter, softened | 250 mL |
| 1 cup | icing sugar | 250 mL |
| 1 | egg | 1 |
| 1 tsp | almond extract | 5 mL |
| 1 tsp | vanilla | 5 mL |
| 2-3/4 cups | all-purpose flour | 675 mL |
| 1 tsp | baking powder | 5 mL |
| 1 tsp | salt | 5 mL |
| 3/4 cup | whole blanched almonds | 175 mL |
| 1 | tube (19 g) red decorator gel | 1 |

1 In bowl, beat together butter, sugar, egg, almond extract and vanilla; beat in flour, baking powder and salt. Cover and refrigerate for 30 minutes.

2 Working with one-quarter of the dough at a time and keeping remaining dough refrigerated, roll heaping teaspoonful (5 mL) into finger shape for each cookie. Press almond firmly into one end for nail. Squeeze in center to create knuckle shape. Using paring knife, make indents in several places to resemble knuckle.

3 Place cookies on lightly greased baking sheets; bake in 325°F (160°C) oven for 20 to 25 minutes or until pale golden. Let cool for 3 minutes.

4 Lift up almond; squeeze red decorator gel onto nail bed and press almond back in place, so gel oozes out from underneath. Remove cookies from baking sheets; let cool on racks.

Makes about 60 cookies.

Gross out unsuspecting friends and family with these totally lifelike shortbread fingers — complete with knuckles, fingernails and drops of blood.

**EQUIPMENT LIST**
- dry measuring cups
- measuring spoons
- bowl
- paring knife
- baking sheets
- wire racks

# North Pole Cupcakes ▶

Your kitchen will bustle with fun — just like Santa's workshop at the North Pole — as you bake up and decorate Santa, Mrs. Claus, the elves and a whole team of reindeer cupcakes.

## EQUIPMENT LIST
• muffin pans for 12 cupcakes
• paper muffin cups or pastry brush
• dry measuring cups
• liquid measuring cup
• measuring spoons
• large bowl
• 2 medium bowls
• small bowls
• electric mixer
• wooden spoons
• wire rack
• palette knife

| 3/4 cup | butter, softened | 175 mL |
|---|---|---|
| 1 cup | granulated sugar | 250 mL |
| 2 | eggs | 2 |
| 1 tsp | vanilla | 5 mL |
| 2 cups | all-purpose flour | 500 mL |
| 1-1/2 tsp | baking powder | 7 mL |
| 1/2 tsp | cinnamon | 2 mL |
| 1/4 tsp | each nutmeg and salt | 1 mL |
| 2/3 cup | milk | 150 mL |
| | Assorted candies, miniature marshmallows and pretzels (see Decorating Cupcakes, p. 81) | |
| | ICING | |
| 1 cup | butter, softened | 250 mL |
| 4 cups | icing sugar | 1 L |
| 2 tbsp | milk | 25 mL |
| | Paste or liquid food coloring | |

1 Line 12 large muffin cups with paper liners or grease lightly; set aside.

2 In large bowl, beat butter with sugar until fluffy. Beat in eggs, one at a time, then vanilla.

3 In separate bowl, stir together flour, baking powder, cinnamon, nutmeg and salt; stir into butter mixture alternately with milk, making three additions of dry ingredients and two of milk. Spoon into muffin cups.

4 Bake in 400°F (200°C) oven for about 25 minutes or until golden brown and tops spring back when lightly touched. Let cool in pan on rack for 5 minutes; transfer to rack and let cool completely. *(Cupcakes can be stored in airtight container for up to 24 hours.)*

5 ICING: In bowl, beat butter until fluffy. Beat in icing sugar alternately with milk, making three additions of icing sugar and two of milk. *(Icing can be refrigerated in airtight container for up to 1 day; beat slightly before using.)*

6 Divide icing among bowls and tint with food coloring as desired (see Decorating Cupcakes, p. 81).

7 Decorate cupcakes as desired with icing, candies, marshmallows and pretzels, increasing amounts as necessary for the number of cupcakes of each type. *(Cupcakes can be covered loosely with plastic wrap and refrigerated for up to 1 day.)*

Makes 12 cupcakes.

**TIP:** Leave the spices out of the cupcakes if you prefer simple white ones.

# DECORATING CUPCAKES

*Determine how many of each character you want to make and tint icing accordingly.*
*You need about 2 tbsp (25 mL) icing to cover 1 cupcake. Add another 1 tbsp (15 mL) to make a hat.*
*Or tint small amounts as you need them. The icing in the recipe makes enough to cover all*
*the cupcakes generously, with allowance for errors and finger licking.*

## FESTIVE SANTA ▼

● Spread top of 1 cupcake with pink icing. Using red icing, spread or pipe shape of hat. Attach white gum ball or miniature marshmallow for pompom and white candies for trim.

● For beard, snip 8 miniature marshmallows into thirds and place on icing. For eyes, nose and mouth, use small candies. (Red ribbon or shoestring licorice can be snipped to make mouth, as can red gumdrops.)

## RED-NOSED REINDEER ◄

● Tint 3 tbsp (50 mL) icing with 1 tsp (5 mL) unsweetened cocoa powder; spread on top of 1 cupcake. For snout, pipe or mound icing into 3/4-inch (2 cm) diameter circle. For nose, use round red candy or gum ball. For eyes, use snipped marshmallow or candies as desired. For antlers, soften 2 pretzels between damp paper towels for 5 minutes; using serrated knife, cut in half lengthwise. (Or use small candy canes for antlers.) To attach, press through icing and into cupcake.

## SNOWMAN WITH SCARF ►

● Spread top of 1 cupcake with untinted icing. For nose, attach candy-coated licorice candy (for carrot nose, choose orange candy-coated licorice candy). For scarf, drape ribbon licorice around cupcake. For eyes and mouth, use small candies.

## MERRY MRS. CLAUS ►

● Spread top of 1 cupcake with pink icing. For hair, snip 7 miniature marshmallows into thirds and arrange on icing. For eyes, nose, mouth and cheeks, use small candies. Add 2 silver dragées for earrings, if you like.

## SANTA'S LITTLE ELF ◄

● Spread top of 1 cupcake with pink icing. For nose, pipe pink icing or attach candy. Using green icing, spread or pipe on hat. Using silver dragées or other candies, trim hat brim and tip. Pipe icing for ears. For eyes and mouth, use small candies.

# Cookie Cottage ▼

It's a whole lot easier to stage a decorating project when you don't have to start from scratch and make all the parts yourself. Look for small cookies in interesting shapes for windows, cobblestones and the door. A bulk food store is often the best place to shop; you can see the cookies unpackaged and buy only as many as you need.

**EQUIPMENT LIST**
- dry measuring cups
- paper towels
- sharp knife
- pastry bag or palette knife
- scissors

| | | |
|---|---|---|
| 1 | graham cracker | 1 |
| 1/3 cup | Meringue Powder Royal Icing (recipe, p. 88) | 75 mL |
| 8 | Nice cookies | 8 |
| 1 | wafer roll or finger cookie | 1 |
| | **DECORATIONS** | |
| | Fruit leather or small rectangular cookie | |
| 1/2 cup | small banana chips (optional) | 125 mL |
| 1/2 cup | Smarties, licorice allsorts and other assorted candies | 125 mL |

1 Wrap damp paper towel around graham cracker; let stand for 10 minutes or until slightly softened. Cut cracker diagonally to make 2 triangles. Set aside to dry.

2 FOR WALLS: Using icing as glue, join 4 of the Nice cookies at 90-degree angles, sugared sides out, to form box. Let dry for 15 minutes.

3 FOR ROOF: Pipe or spread icing on top edge of front and back walls. Place 1 graham cracker triangle, long edge down, on top of each. Pipe icing along top edges of triangles.

4 Starting about 1 inch (2.5 cm) down from top of triangles, place 1 of the Nice cookies along 1 side for bottom roof panel, leaving 1/2-inch (1 cm) overhang at bottom. Repeat on other side.

5 Spread icing on back of remaining Nice cookies. Place 1 on each side of roof, starting at peak and overlapping bottom roof panel by about 1 inch (2.5 cm). Let dry for 1 hour.

6 FOR CHIMNEY: Cut off 1 end of wafer roll on 45-degree angle. Using icing as glue, attach to 1 side of roof.

7 FOR DOOR: Using scissors, cut fruit leather into 1-1/2- x 3/4-inch (4 x 2 cm) rectangle. Using icing as glue, attach to front of cottage.

8 FOR THATCHED ROOF (IF DESIRED): Dab ends of banana chips (if using) with icing to resemble snow. Using icing as glue, attach to roof in overlapping rows, starting at bottom. Decorate with candies as desired.

Makes 1 cottage.

**TIP:** To make a miniature village of 4 small cottages, you need one 400 g package of Nice cookies, 1 batch of Meringue Powder Royal Icing, 4 graham crackers (plus a few extra in case of breakage), 1 piece of fruit leather for doors and about 2 cups (500 mL) assorted candies (plus more for inevitable snacking).

# Jack-in-the-Cookie-Box ▼

| | | |
|---|---|---|
| 1/3 cup | Meringue Powder Royal Icing (recipe, p. 88) | 75 mL |
| 6 | graham crackers | 6 |
| 8 | miniature round cookies (about 3/4 inch/2 cm) | 8 |
| | Assorted small candies | |
| 1 | ice-cream cone | 1 |
| 2 tsp | coarse colored sugar or candy sprinkles | 10 mL |
| 1 | marshmallow | 1 |
| 2 | pretzel sticks | 2 |

**1** FOR BOX BOTTOM AND SIDES: Cut 5-inch (12 cm) square of sturdy cardboard; cover with foil. Using icing as glue, attach flat side of 1 graham cracker to center of cardboard. Pipe or spread icing on board around 3 edges of cookie. Place 3 more crackers upright on board around iced edges to form 3-sided box. Reinforce corners with icing.

**2** FOR BOX BACK AND LID: On piece of waxed paper and using icing as glue, join remaining crackers at 1 long edge. Let dry for at least 1 hour or overnight.

**3** FOR SPRING: Using icing as glue, stack mini round cookies in column. Let dry for at least 1 hour or overnight.

**4** Using icing as glue, decorate box sides, back and lid with assorted small candies as desired.

**5** FOR HEAD: Using serrated knife, gently saw off large end of ice cream cone to make 4-inch (10 cm) long cone. (Marshmallow should fit snugly inside cut end of cone.) Dab tip and cut end with icing; dip both ends into colored sugar. Place on top of marshmallow, fitting marshmallow inside cone slightly.

**6** Using icing as glue, attach small candies for eyes, nose and mouth. Using icing, attach head to top of cookie stack. (You may need to lean head against box or wall to support while drying.) Pipe hair if desired. Let all pieces dry for 1 hour.

**7** Dab icing generously in bottom of box. Place cookie stack on top, pressing gently to attach. Pipe or spread icing along edges of open side of box. Stand box back and lid piece upright and press into position.

**8** Attach pretzel sticks for arms. Let stand for 2 hours or until completely dry. If desired, fill box to brim with small candies.

Makes 1 Jack-in-the-Cookie-Box.

Here's a perfect project for a children's party or get-together. Assemble the boxes and springs ahead of time so the icing glue has time to set — then let the toymakers decorate Jack's box and face as they please.

**EQUIPMENT LIST**
- dry measuring cup
- measuring spoons
- sturdy cardboard
- aluminum foil
- scissors
- waxed paper
- serrated knife
- pastry bag

**TIP:** Place the boxes where desired before filling with candies; moving filled boxes is risky.

# Chocolate Bar House ◀

| 3 lb | icing sugar, sifted | 1.5 kg |
|---|---|---|
| 3 | egg whites (or 5 tbsp/75 mL meringue powder) | 3 |
| 1/2 cup | (approx) water | 125 mL |
| 1 lb | chocolate fingers or chocolate-covered wafers, for walls | 500 g |
| | Assorted candies, for windows, doors and trim | |
| | Chocolate-covered raisins or nuts | |
| | Large chocolate-covered caramel nut bar, for chimney | |
| | Cereal squares | |
| | Plain chocolate bar | |

1 Thoroughly rinse and dry milk cartons. Tape tops closed; secure cartons together with tape and place on large flat platter or upside-down baking sheet.

2 In bowl, mix together sugar, egg whites and enough of the water, 1 tbsp (15 mL) at a time, to make spreadable icing thick enough to act as glue. Using palette knife, spread over sides and tops of milk cartons; spread around base to resemble snow.

3 Coat base of chocolate fingers with a little icing; press onto house to resemble log cabin. Coat backs of assorted candies with icing; press onto walls for windows and doors. Press chocolate-covered raisins along corners of walls; press onto "snow" base for sidewalk.

4 Using icing as glue, attach large chocolate-covered caramel nut bar onto side of wall for chimney. Starting at bottom of each roof and layering toward top, attach cereal squares to resemble thatched roof.

5 Stand 2 chocolate fingers in snow for shed posts. Using icing as glue, attach plain chocolate bar on top for shed roof. Trim roofs with icing and candies as desired.

Makes 1 house.

With this delightful creation from food writer and cooking-school teacher Bonnie Stern, you can turn yourself into a chocolate-bar architect and build your dream house. The shape, size and look depend on the cartons you begin with, as well as the candy bars, cereal shapes or cookies you choose for decorating.

**EQUIPMENT LIST**
- 1 (1 L) milk carton
- 1 (500 mL) milk carton
- tape
- sifter
- liquid measuring cup
- flat platter or baking sheet
- bowl
- palette knife

**TIP:** Rinse out the milk cartons very well before starting the project and allow them to air-dry overnight. Seal them closed again for an even roof.

# Gingerbread Carousel ▶

Home economist Jill Snider was the mastermind behind this charming holiday merry-go-round. You can make all the pieces one day and store them for construction a few days later. Leave plenty of time; you'll need a whole afternoon for assembly, as pieces need to dry and harden as you go along.

**EQUIPMENT LIST**
- dry measuring cups
- parchment paper
- rolling pin
- plate or cake pan
- knife
- rimless baking sheets
- wire rack
- cookie cutters
- pastry bag, plain tip and #402 medium star tip
- serrated knife
- elastic band
- cake board or tray
- palette knife

| | | |
|---|---|---|
| 2 | batches Gingerbread Dough (recipe, p. 88) | 2 |
| 2 | batches Royal Icing (recipe, p. 88) | 2 |
| | CAROUSEL DECORATIONS | |
| 19 | candy sticks, 5 inches (12 cm) long | 19 |
| 7 | gumdrop rings | 7 |
| 1/4 cup | mini multicolored candies | 50 mL |
| 1/4 cup | green candy sprinkles | 50 mL |
| 24 | gum balls | 24 |
| 1-1/2 oz | candy-coated milk-chocolate rounds (about 50) | 40 g |
| 1 | large gum ball | 1 |
| 6 | gumdrops | 6 |
| | DECORATIONS FOR CUTOUTS | |
| 1 cup | assorted candies (silver dragées, colored mini chips, mini jelly beans, gumdrops) | 250 mL |

1 Working with half a batch of the chilled Gingerbread Dough at a time, roll out dough directly on parchment paper to 1/4-inch (5 mm) thickness. Cut into 9-inch (23 cm) circle, using plate or cake pan as guide. Repeat with 2 more halves of dough to make 3 circles.

2 Place paper and circles on baking sheets; bake in 350°F (180°C) oven for 20 to 25 minutes or until dry and firm to the touch. Let cool on pan on rack.

3 On well-floured surface, roll out remaining dough to same thickness. Using floured cookie cutters, cut out shapes as follows, gathering scraps of dough from all batches and rerolling dough once:
- 13 round (1-1/2-inch/4 cm) cookies;
- 6 round (1-1/2-inch/4 cm) cookies with 1/2-inch (1 cm) round hole cut from centers;
- 6 reindeer (4 inches/10 cm);
- 6 small gingerbread people (2 inches/5 cm).

4 Place larger figures on one greased or parchment paper-lined baking sheet, smaller figures and circles on another. Bake in 350°F (180°C) oven for 15 to 20 minutes for large, 8 to 15 minutes for small, or until dry and firm to the touch. Let cool on pan on rack.

5 DECORATIONS FOR CUTOUTS: Using piping bag fitted with plain tip, pipe Royal Icing around edge of reindeer to outline. Glue on silver dragées or other candies with icing. Let dry. Decorate gingerbread people with icing and candies as desired. Let dry.

6 CAROUSEL DECORATIONS: With serrated knife, trim candy sticks to same height. Moisten 1 stick with water; surround with 6 candy sticks to form pillar, securing with elastic band or twist tie. Remove elastic band when dry. Smear ends with icing sugar; set aside.

7 For base, spread 2 tbsp (25 mL) icing on 12-inch (30 cm) round cake board or flat-bottomed tray; place 1 of the gingerbread rounds on top. Spread with 2 tbsp (25 mL) icing; cover with second gingerbread round. Spread top with 1/3 cup (75 mL) icing.

8 Using more icing as glue, stick 6 round cookies with holes, flat side down, around edge of base 1/2 inch (1 cm) from edge. Glue gumdrop rings over holes. Fill holes to overflowing with icing. Sprinkle mini multicolored candies around cookies to cover base, pressing to adhere.

9 Using #402 medium star tip, pipe large rosette on center of base. Press candy stick into icing in each hole of gumdrop rings. Press candy pillar in center of rosette. Let dry, about 1 hour.

10 Meanwhile, for roof, spread 1/3 cup (75 mL) icing over remaining gingerbread base; sprinkle with green candy sprinkles, pressing to adhere.

*Recipe continued on page 88*

# Gingerbread Carousel (continued)

Using pastry bag fitted with #402 medium star tip, pipe icing into rosettes around edge. Place gum ball on each. Set aside.

11 Pipe icing onto top of each candy stick; place decorated roof on top. Using icing as glue, place reindeer on candy stick poles with gumdrop bases. Let dry, about 30 minutes.

12 Using #402 medium star tip, pipe rosettes around edge of base; top each with milk chocolate round. Pipe rosettes around top of base.

13 Using icing as glue, stack together 13 round cookies; glue to center of roof. Glue candy sticks from top of stack to edge of roof, aligning with each candy stick below. Decorate top of cookie stack with gumdrop ring and large gum ball.

14 Using icing as glue, attach gingerbread people to roof, placing gumdrop behind each as support. Let dry for 24 hours before moving.

Makes 1 carousel.

# Gingerbread Dough

You'll need two batches to make the carousel, with enough to munch on while piecing it together.

## EQUIPMENT LIST
- dry measuring cups
- liquid measuring cup
- measuring spoons
- medium bowl
- large bowl
- electric mixer
- wooden spoon
- plastic wrap

| 1 cup | shortening | 250 mL |
|---|---|---|
| 1 cup | packed dark brown sugar | 250 mL |
| 1/4 cup | fancy molasses | 50 mL |
| 1/4 cup | milk | 50 mL |
| 3-1/4 cups | all-purpose flour | 800 mL |
| 2 tsp | baking soda | 10 mL |
| 2 tsp | cinnamon | 10 mL |
| 2 tsp | ground ginger | 10 mL |
| 3/4 tsp | ground cloves | 4 mL |
| 1/2 tsp | salt | 2 mL |

1 In large bowl, beat together shortening, brown sugar, molasses and milk until smooth and creamy. In separate bowl, stir together flour, baking soda, cinnamon, ginger, cloves and salt; using wooden spoon, stir into shortening mixture in three additions just until smooth dough forms. Gather into ball; turn out onto lightly floured surface.

2 Divide in half; form into 1/2-inch (1 cm) thick discs. Wrap each in plastic wrap and refrigerate for at least 3 hours or overnight. Let stand at room temperature for 15 minutes before rolling.

Makes 1 batch of dough.

## ICINGS FOR COOKIE PROJECTS
*Use these icings to build and ice the various gingerbread and cookie creations in this chapter, as indicated in individual recipes.*

### Royal Icing
● In large bowl, beat 3 egg whites with 1/2 tsp (2 mL) cream of tartar at high speed until frothy. Gradually beat in 4 cups sifted icing sugar for about 4 minutes, beating until very stiff. Keep covered with damp cloth to prevent drying out.
**Makes about 2 cups (500 mL).**

### Meringue Powder Royal Icing
● In bowl, beat 1/4 cup (50 mL) water with 2 tbsp (25 mL) meringue powder until combined; gradually beat in 2-1/3 cups (575 mL) icing sugar for about 4 minutes or until very stiff. Cover with damp cloth to prevent drying out.
**Makes 1-1/2 cups (375 mL).**

# Gingerbread Picture Frames

| | | |
|---|---|---|
| 1/3 cup | shortening | 75 mL |
| 1/3 cup | packed brown sugar | 75 mL |
| 1 | egg | 1 |
| 1/3 cup | fancy molasses | 75 mL |
| 2-1/4 cups | all-purpose flour | 550 mL |
| 3/4 tsp | ground ginger | 4 mL |
| 1/2 tsp | cinnamon | 2 mL |
| 1/4 tsp | each salt, baking soda and ground allspice | 1 mL |
| | Meringue Powder Royal Icing (recipe, p. 88) | |
| | Assorted candies | |

1 Lightly grease 2 of the baking sheets and set aside.

2 In large bowl, beat shortening with brown sugar until fluffy; beat in egg and molasses. In separate bowl, stir together flour, ginger, cinnamon, salt, baking soda and allspice; using wooden spoon, stir into molasses mixture until soft dough forms.

3 Gather into ball and turn out onto lightly floured surface. Divide in half; press each half into rectangle about 1 inch (2.5 cm) thick. Wrap in plastic wrap and refrigerate for at least 2 hours or until chilled. (Dough can be refrigerated for up to 1 week.)

4 Using photo of arch frame (right) as guide, and keeping in mind size of photos, draw frame on light cardboard and cut out. You can also make stars, houses, trees, rounds or other holiday shapes using larger and smaller cookie cutters.

5 Working with one piece of dough at a time, roll out between parchment or waxed paper into 12- x 8-inch (30 x 20 cm) rectangle; peel off top sheet of paper. Lift onto inverted baking sheet; freeze for 30 minutes or until hard.

6 Using tip of sharp knife, trace pattern pieces onto dough and cut out. Transfer cutouts to prepared pans, reserving scraps; peel away paper. Using straw, pierce hole in dough at center top if desired for hanging. Refrigerate for 5 minutes before baking.

7 Reroll scraps as above; cut out more frames. Make small decorative cutouts from remaining scraps as desired.

8 Bake in 350°F (180°C) oven for about 12 minutes or until golden and firm to the touch. Let cool completely on pan on rack. (Gingerbread can be stored in airtight containers for up to 2 weeks.)

9 Divide and tint Meringue Powder Royal Icing if desired. Spread or pipe decoratively onto frames. Decorate as desired with candies and small gingerbread cutouts. Cover remaining icing with plastic wrap and refrigerate. Let frames stand for at least 8 hours or until completely dry.

10 Trim photos slightly larger than openings in frames. Dot edges of photos with reserved icing; place frames over photos, pressing gently to adhere. Let dry completely. For each, thread ribbon through hole and tie bow to hang if desired.

Makes 8 arch frames plus various smaller decorations.

Frame an assortment of snapshots or a portrait of you with Santa using these seasonally sweet do-it-yourself frames. Hang your frame with a pretty ribbon, or prop it on a small easel.

**EQUIPMENT LIST**
- 3 baking sheets
- pastry brush
- dry measuring cups
- small bowl
- table knife
- electric mixer
- measuring spoons
- plastic wrap
- parchment paper or waxed paper
- rolling pin
- cookie cutters
- small sharp knife
- straw
- metal lifter
- wire rack
- scissors
- ribbon or easels

# The Contributors

## Photography Credits

LAURA ARSIE: cover photograph of Elizabeth Baird; photograph of the Canadian Living Test Kitchen staff.

FRED BIRD: pages 12, 31, 39, 48, 55, 59, 60.

DOUGLAS BRADSHAW: pages 15, 76, 77, 78.

CHRISTOPHER CAMPBELL: pages 22, 25, 73.

DAN COUTO: page 79.

YVONNE DUIVENVOORDEN: page 64.

FRANK GRANT: page 20.

VINCENT NOGUCHI: pages 16, 72.

MICHAEL WARING: pages 19, 26, 84.

ROBERT WIGINGTON: front cover; pages 3, 4, 7, 8, 32, 34, 40, 43, 45, 46, 62, 71, 75, 81, 82, 83, 87, 89.

*In the Canadian Living Test Kitchen. Clockwise from left: Elizabeth Baird (food director), Heather Howe (manager), Susan Van Hezewijk, Emily Richards, Donna Bartolini (associate food director), Daphna Rabinovitch (associate food director) and Jennifer MacKenzie.*

## Special Thanks

Praise and thanks go to the talented and enthusiastic team who put together *Canadian Living's Best Kids in the Kitchen*. First, to the Canadian Living Test Kitchen staff. As professionals in the food world, they know how much pleasure comes from cooking well. Our staff includes home economists Emily Richards, Susan Van Hezewijk, Jennifer MacKenzie and manager Heather Howe, plus associate food directors Daphna Rabinovitch and Donna Bartolini. Nobody gets more of a thrill from constructing a dinosaur out of cake layers and icing or tackling serious construction with slabs of gingerbread than this group of usually grown-up cooks!

Appreciation goes also to our valued food writers (noted above), especially Bonnie Stern and Pam Collacott, whose kids' recipes are so important to this collection. In their cooking schools (Bonnie's in Toronto and Pam's in North Gower, south of Ottawa), they spread the word that cooking is fun, an incredibly important life skill and a wonderful way to share heritage and knowledge as well as delicious tastes.

Joining those who deserve recognition are *Canadian Living's* managing editor Susan Antonacci, editorial assistant Olga Goncalves, senior editor Julia Armstrong, our copy department under Michael Killingsworth and our art department guided by Cate Cochran. Special thanks to our meticulous senior food editor, Beverley Renahan, for her high standards of consistency and accuracy and to editor-in-chief Bonnie Cowan and publisher Caren King for their support.

There are others to thank, too. On the visual side — our photographers (noted above); prop stylists Maggi Jones, Janet Walkinshaw, Shelly Tauber, Bridget Sargeant and Susan Doherty-Hannaford who provide the backgrounds, dishes and embellishments for the luscious food photos; and food stylists Kate Bush, Ruth Gangbar, Debby Charendoff Moses, Lucie Richard, Olga Truchan, Jennifer McLagan, Jill Snider, Sharon Dale and Kathy Robertson who do the creative cooking, arranging and garnishing of recipes.

Book designers Gord Sibley and Dale Vokey are responsible for the splendid new kid-friendly design of this *Best* cookbook. Thanks also to Albert Cummings, president of Madison Press Books.

Working with Wanda Nowakowska, associate editorial director at Madison, is always a pleasure — certainly for her high standard of workmanship and creativity that have made the whole *Best* series so user-friendly and attractive, but also for her calm and always thoughtful, kind and generous nature. Thanks also to Tina Gaudino, Donna Chong, Rosemary Hillary and others at Madison Press Books.

Appreciation for their contribution at Random House is extended to Duncan Shields (mass marketing sales manager), Mary Jane Boreham, members of the marketing and publicity departments — Kathleen Bain, Pat Cairns, Sheila Kay, Cathy Paine, Maria Medeiros and Deborah Bjorgan — and to president and publisher David Kent.

*Elizabeth Baird*

# Index

*C*heck it out!
Over 100 awesome
recipes guaranteed to
get kids cooking.

Trust Canadian Living to bring you the **BEST!**